Martini Nel

Decorate with motifs

Human & Rousseau
Cape Town Pretoria Johannesburg

To God be the glory,
Great things He has done!

This book is dedicated to Adri, Martinette and Adriaan

A sincere thank you to the following persons for their contributions: Leonie Avenant, Hermann Chandler, Salomé Cilliers, Héléne Krugmann, Via Laurie, Di Donnelly, Eileen de Lange of Craft, Gifts and Things, Jackie Niemand, Martie Groenewald, Melanie Niemand, Ronel Visser and especially also to Janita van der Merwe.
Hand-coloured fabric and thread were supplied by Quilt Fabrics & NeedleArt.
Thank you to Screen T in Bellville for baking the fabric painting articles.
My thanks also to Anelma Ruschioni and Lesley Krige of Human & Rousseau, Colin and Lindsay Young, as well as Eileen Snowball and Neil Corder.

Copyright © 2001 by Martini Nel
First published in 2001 by Human & Rousseau (Pty) Ltd,
Design Centre, 179 Loop Street, Cape Town
Translation by Pat Barton
Photography by Neil Corder
Styling by Eileen Snowball
Motifs by Wiekie Theron
Line drawings by Elmarié van der Merwe
for *Create your own Soft Furnishings* by Martini Nel
Typography and cover design by Susan Bloemhof
Text electronically prepared and set in 10 pt on 13 pt Avant Garde
by ALINEA STUDIO, Cape Town
Colour separations by Paarl Colour, Paarl
Printed in China through Colorcraft Ltd., Hong Kong

ISBN 0 7981 4135 2

No part of this book may be reproduced or transmitted in any form or by any means, electronic or mechanical, or by photo-copying, recording or microfilming, or stored in any retrieval system without the written permission of the publisher

Contents

Basic techniques 4

   Machine appliqué 4
   Embroidery 4
   Fabric painting 5
   Flour (or batik) technique 6
   Painting on wood 7
   Painting on glass and porcelain 7
   Stencilling 8
   Stamping 9
   Decoupage 10
   Plaster ornaments and decorations 11

Themes

Africa 12
Leaves 14
Shells 16
Sea 18
Animals 20
Flowers 22
Topiary trees 24
Cacti, herbs and lavender 26
Vegetables 28
Fruit 30

Motifs 32

Basic techniques

Craft work has a calming influence on most people. In addition, it is useful for decorating your home and all kinds of pretty and practical articles. The possibilities are endless.

Combine the technique you decide on with a motif and colours of your choice to create something unique for your home, or as a gift for someone special.

Some of the most popular techniques are discussed briefly here, but feel free to experiment with other techniques and motifs.

Machine appliqué

Appliqué consists of stitching pieces of fabric to background fabric to make a motif. (You can also stitch existing motifs to background fabric.)

You will need: a suitable pattern; a pencil or pen; fabric; matching thread; iron-on appliqué paper with glue on both sides; and basic needlework requisites.

Method:

- Draw the pattern on one side of the appliqué paper.
- Cut out the pattern pieces and iron them to the wrong sides of the various fabrics, with the written-on side facing the fabric.
- Cut out the pattern pieces from the fabric.
  Note: The order in which the pattern pieces are attached is very important. Lay out the cut-out pattern and number the pattern pieces. The bottom pieces are ironed on first, and the other pieces placed on top. Where pieces meet, a seam allowance must be added to the bottom pattern piece, which slides in under the top piece, so that they overlap.
- Pin or tack the first pattern piece in position on the background fabric. Iron it on. Place the remaining pieces on the fabric, in the correct order, and iron them on too.
- Now stitch the pattern pieces, using a narrow zigzag stitch or satin stitch. Stitch the bottom pattern pieces first. Remember to have the same colour thread on the bottom and top spools. The machine's tension is usually set so that the bottom thread is slightly tighter than the top thread. This ensures that the bottom thread will not be visible on the right side.

Tip: Before you stitch the pattern pieces in position, test the stitch length and width on a piece of leftover fabric. Make sure that at least two thirds of the stitch is on the pattern piece and the rest is on the background, otherwise the pattern piece could fray with time.

Embroidery

Embroidery is very popular for household articles, and even on clothes. You can make attractive articles using only a few basic embroidery stitches.

Combine various stitches to attach motifs.

Back stitch

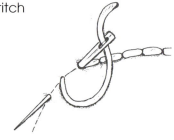

Bullion knot

French knot

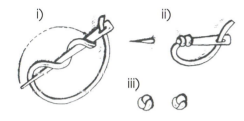

Stem stitch

Lazy daisy stitch

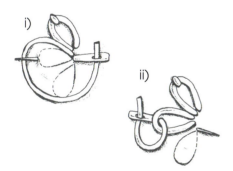

Chain stitch

Fly stitch

 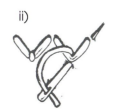

Fabric painting

There are a number of fabric painting techniques. You can paint large abstract designs and designs with little detail, or delicate designs with a lot of detail.

Experiment with various techniques to find out which one you like best. Only a few methods, those used for articles in this book, are explained here.

For fabric painting you will need the following: unbleached calico or any other suitable fabric; soft pencil or marker (water-soluble ink); fabric paint in different colours, extender; brushes and outliner or permanent (indelible) markers.

Method:

- Draw the motif you want to paint on to the fabric. Use a marker that has water-soluble ink (not the kind that disappears after a while) or a soft pencil.

    Note: Tailor's tracing paper is also suitable, but make sure that the contrast between the paper and the colour of the fabric is sufficient to show the pattern clearly.

    The design can also be cut from stick-on paper (Contact). Stick the design to the fabric and trace all around the outline of the design. You can use masking tape for small designs, such as leaves, butterflies and flowers.

Before tracing a motif, you have to draw it on paper using a black pen. Place the fabric in position over the design and keep the design in place with masking tape. Use a light table, a glass-topped table with a switched-on electric lamp underneath, or work against a window so that you can see the design at the back better.

Tip: Stick strips of masking tape in position and paint over them for a neat chequered effect, or for stripes.

- Now paint the design in the colours of your choice. Shade in a darker colour to form shadows and a lighter colour for light patches.

  Scrape off paint with the back of a brush, a knitting needle or a sosatie skewer to add detail to the design.

  First paint the parts of the design that are the "furthest" from you and, lastly, paint the parts right in front.

  You can paint the background before painting the motif, or after the motif has been completed.

Tip: If you have to paint an extensive background, you can thin the paint with more extender to make it easier to apply. Practise the various methods on a piece of leftover fabric to find out which one suits you best.

- Finish off the design with a liner after the design and background have been painted, if you wish. Use a colour of your choice to draw around the outline of the motif. It can be the same, a darker, or a contrasting colour. Popular colours for lining are gold, silver, green, white and black. A combination of two colours can also be used for a single motif. For example, outline the motif with black and then with gold.

  You can use a special liner in a small bottle with a nozzle. You can also use permanent (indelible) markers, or a very thin paint brush and fabric paint. Outlining neatly with a brush is very time-consuming, so I prefer to use a liner, fabric-painting pens or permanent (indelible) markers.

- Allow the paint to dry completely – it should preferably have been in place on the article for at least 24 hours – then heat-seal it to ensure that the paint will remain permanently on the fabric. There are various techniques:

  The easiest and most reliable is to take the articles to professionals, such as a silk-screening company, and have them **baked** in a special oven. This is inexpensive and extremely reliable. You can be sure that the articles have reached the same temperature all over, and that there will not be parts that will wash out or fade quickly.

  You can also **iron** the article. Place a clean piece of fabric over the painted part and iron it thoroughly with a hot iron (do not steam-iron it). The iron should be kept on an area for about 10 seconds to ensure that the heat gets through sufficiently.

  The article can also be placed in a **tumble dryer**, set to a hot temperature, and left for about 45 minutes.

Flour (or batik) technique

You will need the following for this easy fabric-painting technique: flour; water; a plastic bottle with a pointed spout and smallish hole; unbleached calico, marker with blue water-soluble ink; fabric paint and brushes.

Method:

- Mix one part flour with one part water to make a thick liquid. An easy way to test the thickness is to allow a few drops to drip on to a leftover piece of fabric. If the drops remain, half-rounded, in position, the mixture is thick enough. If the drops run into one another or flatten too much against the background, the mixture is too thin. Experiment until you get the right thickness.

Tip: To make it easier to remove the dry flour later, add one teaspoon of alum to the mixture for each cup of flour.

- Pour the flour mixture into the plastic bottle. (The bigger the hole, the wider the pattern lines will be. For smaller designs you need a narrow line, but the lines can be wider for large designs.)
- Draw the design on to the fabric, using a marker with blue water-soluble ink. Trace the lines of the design, using the flour mixture in the squeeze bottle.

    You can also draw a freehand design on the fabric, using the flour mixture; or you can draw your design on paper, using a black pen, then place it under the fabric and trace the design, using the flour mixture.

    If you are working on a large design, or want to repeat a motif, be very careful when moving the fabric, so that you do not smear the flour mixture. It would be better to wait until the first lines have dried before applying more of the flour mixture.
- Allow the article to dry completely.
- Now paint the design in the usual way, in colours of your choice.
- Wait until the painted part has dried completely, then remove the flour by scratching it off carefully, using an egg lifter. If the painted article has already been heat-treated, you can wash out the flour or moisten it with a damp cloth and then scrape it off with an egg-lifter.

Painting on wood

Various kinds of paint can be used on wood. Craft paint appears to be the most popular and is widely available. It is sold in handy smaller packs, in a wide variety of colours. Acrylic PVA paint is also suitable.

To make sure that the paint you want to use will look attractive, test it on the underside of the article.

To paint on wood, you will need: suitable paint; brushes; fine sandpaper; and a damp cloth.

Method:

- Make sure that the surface of the wood is smooth by sanding it with fine sandpaper. Wipe it clean with a damp cloth to ensure that no wood dust remains.
- Cover the article with a coat of paint in the desired colour. Wait until it has dried, then paint on another coat. Allow to dry completely. Sand the article carefully, using fine sandpaper, if it is not smooth.
- Decide where you want the motif or motifs to be placed and draw them lightly on the article, using a pencil.
- Now paint the motif in the colours of your choice. Shade in darker colours to form shadows and lighter colours for light patches. Use a small, dry brush to shade colours in gradually.
- Allow the paint to dry completely.

Painting on glass and porcelain

Hand-painted crockery is very popular and makes an ordinary article special.

There are various methods for painting crockery. Only one is discussed here, as it is easy and produces a long-lasting result.

It's a good idea to paint around the rim only

(not in the centre) of articles such as plates, which take a lot of punishment from knives. Doing this will ensure that the article will not be damaged. If the article is going to be used decoratively, however – such as a plate used only for biscuits – the entire surface may be decorated.

To paint on glass and porcelain, you will need: glass paint – for this technique, the imported French kind available from art supplies shops and craft shops, is best; fine brushes; and an oven.

Method for painting on glass:

- Draw the design you want to paint on to paper.
- Cut out the design and fix it in the correct position on the inside of the glass, using masking tape.
- Paint the design on the outside of the glass.
  If you paint something and you are not happy with it, you can wipe off the paint with a damp cloth; provided that it has not yet been baked. If you simply want to remove a small mark or stripe before baking the article, scratch it off carefully using a small, sharp knife.
- Place the article in a cold oven and heat the oven to 160 °C. Bake the article for about 35 minutes, or according to the paint manufacturer's instructions, and allow to cool completely.

Method for painting on porcelain:

- If you want to paint a simple motif, you can draw it lightly on the porcelain article, using a pencil. You do not have to draw in all the detail; just the basic pencil lines to serve as guide.
- If you want to draw a larger motif, you can first draw the motif's outline on paper. Cut it out carefully, just inside the pencil lines. Using small pieces of wonder putty (Prestik), stick the paper pattern carefully in position on the porcelain. (You could also use stick-on paper.) Trace around the motif with pencil and remove the paper motif.
- Paint the motif and bake the article as described above.

Tip: You can first paint the outline and bake the article in the oven, then, as soon as it has cooled, paint more detail on the design, but you must bake it again.

Stencilling

Stencilling is a simple, but very effective, way to depict designs in various paint techniques. It can thus be used for fabric painting, painting on wood, painting on glass and many other techniques.

To make a stencil, you will need: a craft knife or scalpel; a cutting block or other surface that will not be damaged by the knife; pencil and paper; a permanent (indelible) marker that can write on plastic; and transparent plastic, such as that used for overhead projectors or old X-ray plates.

To use a stencil, you will need: stencil brushes, sponges or a sponge roller; the appropriate type of paint for the specific technique you want to use, as well as the other requisites for the specific technique.

How to cut out a stencil:

- Draw the stencil design on paper. Make sure that there are enough "bridges" in the design. These are the thin strips that are not cut out. If there are not enough bridges, the brush will slide easily under the design and the motif will not have clearly defined outlines.
- Place the design under transparent plastic and trace the lines on it. You could also make a copy of the original design and stick it under the transparent plastic with masking tape.
  Note: The design should not be placed too close to the edge of the plastic; if it is, you could easily paint over the edge when you stencil it.
- Use a very sharp craft knife to cut the design from the plastic. Take care not to let the knife slip and make unnecessary cuts in the plastic. Press the plastic down firmly with your free hand while you cut.

Tip: If you are going to use more than one colour of paint, you may have to cut out a number of stencils for the various colours of paint that you are going to use.

Method:

- Place the cut-out stencil on the surface on which you want to place the motif. Stick it in position with masking tape to ensure that it will not move while you are working – you can also use a special stencil glue.
- Pour a little paint into a suitable container.
- Put the brush, sponge or sponge roller into the paint. Make sure that there is not too much paint on the brush, sponge or roller. To get rid of excess paint, you could press the brush on an old piece of paper.
- Paint the opening in the stencil that you want painted. Take care not to let the paint seep in under the plastic edge. The brush could also be pressed on the surface using light pressing movements. This will create a splattering effect.

    You can shade in a second colour, if you wish. In this way you can obtain light and shadow effects on the stencilled motifs.

    Note: It is very important to remember that the stencil must not be shifted while the paint is still wet.
- Lift the stencil carefully in order to remove it.

    If there is wet paint on the underside of the stencil, wipe it off before sticking it in position again.

Stamping

Stamping is versatile and very easy. You can use bought stamps or make simple stamps yourself.

Bought stamps usually have a lot of detail and can produce attractive results. There's a wide variety available commercially.

You can make a simple stamp from a cut potato. Draw a simple motif lightly on the cut surface of the potato and cut away the parts around the motif, using a small, sharp knife. You could also cut detail into the motif. The motif should stand out about 1 cm.

Another way to make stamps is to cut sponge into simple shapes and use them as stamps.

Stamps can also be cut from rubber erasers. If you have a sharp craft knife, you can cut out delicate motifs.

Stamping can be done on various surfaces. In addition to a stamp, you also need the appropriate type of paint, and the other requisites for the specific technique to be used.

You can use a stamp pad for some stamps, but you could also apply the paint with a small brush or sponge roller.

Method:

- Press the stamp on the stamp pad or apply the paint with a small brush or sponge roller. In both cases, make sure that the stamp is covered with paint, but that there is not too much. Make sure that holes and grooves do not get paint in them.
- Press the stamp on the surface. Make sure that you press it evenly so that the entire stamp pattern is "printed". It often happens that part of the stamp is not pressed hard enough, and so one part of the motif is lighter than the rest.
- Allow the paint to dry and decorate or colour in the motif as desired.

Decoupage

Decoupage is a very old decorative technique which has once again become extremely popular. It involves the pasting and sealing of motifs (usually paper) on a background, usually wood. Decoupage could also be used to apply motifs to, for example, porcelain, glass, candles and soap.

Although ordinary gift wrap is often used, special paper, made specifically for decoupage, is also available. You could also cut out pretty motifs from fabric.

There are a number of ways to do decoupage, depending on what you have available. To paste the motif to the background, you can use wallpaper paste, podge, thinned white wood glue or craft glue. You will also need brushes and a small rubber roller (available from art supplies stores and craft stores).

You can use colourless, matte or gloss varnish.

If the decoupage is to be done on wood, you may also need the following: fine sandpaper; a damp cloth and paint for the background.

How to prepare a wooden article for decoupage:

- Sand the wood with fine sandpaper.
- Wipe it clean with a damp cloth to ensure that no wood dust remains.
- Use craft paints, acrylic PVA or any other good-quality paint and paint the article carefully.

You can give the article a **colour-washed look** by applying thinned paint unevenly, so that the wood grain shows through. To thin the paint, mix two parts paint with one part water and add a few drops of dishwashing liquid.

To create a **two-colour washed look**, first paint the article with a thin base coat. Then add a second colour in the same way as for a colour-washed look.

Use unthinned paint to create a **neat painted look**. Apply one coat of paint. Wait until it is dry, then sand it evenly with sandpaper. Wipe off all the wood dust with a damp cloth. Apply another coat of paint. If necessary, sand it again lightly once the paint is dry. The article is now ready for decoupage.

Tip: If desired, decorate the background with various paint techniques, such as painting detail around the decoupage motif.

Method:

- Spread a thin coat of podge on the paper motif you are going to use and wait until it dries. (This simply strengthens the paper and is not always necessary.)
- Cut the motif out carefully. Make sure that you cut away all the excess background paper.
- Spread a thin coat of glue on the article, in the position where the motif is to be placed. Place the motif carefully in position and roll out all the air bubbles with the small rubber roller. Allow to dry.
- If you want to add extra detail to the article, you can do so now. If you add it after all the coats of podge have been applied, you will have to add another thin coat to ensure that the pen marks or paint will not smudge when you paint on the varnish.
- Apply one thin coat of podge, working in one direction only. A flat sponge brush, available from art supplies shops, is ideal for this purpose. Allow to dry slightly.

- Add another thin coat of podge, this time in the opposite direction. Apply about eight coats of podge in this manner.
- Wait until completely dry, then sand the podge until smooth with fine water paper. If unevenness builds up between the layers, you can also sand this carefully.

  The reason the article is sanded is to make the motif, pasted to the background, level with the background so that it looks as if it is part of the original article and not pasted on later. The total number of coats applied to the decoupage article is your choice. Usually, about 10 coats are applied, but in extreme cases there can be as many as 30 coats.
- Now varnish the article. If necessary, you can apply a second coat of varnish.

Plaster ornaments and decorations

Plaster ornaments and decorations are quick and easy to make. A variety of moulds is available commercially, but you could also use plastic chocolate moulds.

Plaster decorations are not very durable, so always make a few extra in case of breakages. Plaster also varies in quality: Yellowstone is stronger than ordinary plaster and is recommended for this reason. Various materials can be added to the plaster to make it harder – ask your hardware dealer.

To make plaster ornaments, you will need the following: moulds; plaster; a plastic dish and paint (spray or ordinary paint).

Method:

- Pour one part of water in a plastic dish. Add about two parts plaster and stir the mixture until it forms a thickish liquid. (If it hardens too quickly, add a little less plaster next time.)
- Pour the plaster quickly but carefully into the mould. Shake the mould slightly to remove any air bubbles that might have formed, and to ensure that the plaster lies evenly in the moulds. If the plaster flows slightly over the edge of the mould, you can remove it carefully with a wet cloth.
- Wait until the plaster is hard, then press it carefully out of the mould. Neaten the edge of the plaster mould with a small, sharp knife if an ugly, sharp edge has formed. Leave in a warm place, or in the sun, until the plaster has dried completely.
- Spray or paint the articles in the desired colour. First paint the article underneath, then turn it right side up once the base has dried and paint the rest.

Tip: If you are making a plaster ornament to affix to a candle, place a drawing pin in the plaster before it has set, so that all you have to press into the candle later is the point of the drawing pin. A curtain ring can be positioned in the wet plaster for a serviette ring.

Africa

Africa and its wild animals hold a unique charm, and articles decorated with African motifs are now more popular than ever. For a long time now, not only hunters have wanted to decorate their homes with Africa's animals.
Simple designs, such as black zebra stripes against a white background, can be very effective. On the other hand, rich earthy colours such as ochre, camel and rust brown give a room warmth. Use paint, stamps, stencils or decoupage to create the dramatic and characteristic motifs of Africa on articles made from fabric, wood and glass.

This striking picture frame is very easy to make. The wooden frame was first painted white. Then black stripes were painted, freehand, over the white to resemble zebra stripes. Ostrich eggs look like works of art after motifs were painted on them, using black paint.

Wild animal tracks, applied with a stencil, decorate this old tray which was first sanded and painted. To make the simple but effective coasters for glasses and coffee mugs, decoupage animal and animal skin motifs were applied to wooden squares.

Zebra and camel motifs were "printed" on these pot holders, using a bought stamp and fabric paint. Details such as grass were painted on by hand. The leopard head motif on the cushion was painted with fabric paint, and the animal skin motifs around the edge were stencilled.

Tips

- Decorate a variety of picture frames by painting or stencilling simple motifs such as animal skins or animal tracks on to them. Group the frames together on a table or shelf as a focal point.

- Use animal motif stamps to create a striking African tablecloth or place mats. Children can also join in on this project.

- Use a painted ostrich egg as a candle holder, if the hole in the egg is large enough. Cut the bottom of an ordinary candle slightly smaller, using a small, sharp knife, and place it in the ostrich egg. Bend a spiral-shaped stand from wire to support the egg.

- Make a variety of cushions decorated with African motifs and group them on a bench or scatter them on the floor in front of the fireplace.

- Paint zebra motifs on an ordinary pot plant container to incorporate pot plants into the African theme.

- Paint or stamp animal motifs on an ordinary lampshade to make it more appealing.

Leaves

When the first spring leaves appear in beautifully bright shades of green, we feel the need to make everything around us clean and new. One of the most wonderful places to be on a hot summer's day is in the shade of a lush green tree. Around you, you will see every conceivable shade of green; green that yields to brown, yellow, orange and even wine-red in autumn. The variety of leaf shapes, colours and textures is a rich source of inspiration. And do not forget about flower petals! The leaf theme fits into almost every room: on a cushion in the bedroom or sitting room, or on a cover in the kitchen. Use dried leaves or leaf motifs to decorate your home!

Dried autumn leaves were pasted on to this terracotta pot plant holder, then sealed with three layers of podge. The cushions were stencilled with leaf motifs, using different colours of fabric paint.

A pretty compound leaf was pasted on to handmade paper and framed. The broad wooden frame was colour-washed with white paint. Leaves from the different seasons decorate the other picture frame. Pressed spring and autumn leaves were pasted around the edge and sealed with a coat of varnish

Tips

- Collect autumn leaves and dry them. Store them in a safe place for use throughout the rest of the year.

- Create a leaf theme in your kitchen by painting, stencilling or embroidering the motifs on the toaster cover on to other articles, such as cloths, place mats and curtains.

- Laminate pretty, flat, dried leaves in 10 cm x 10 cm squares and use them as coasters for glasses.

- If you picked up leaves during a special outing or trip, you can dry and frame them as a memento. Write the place and date collected on the background paper, following the outline of the leaf, so that the writing goes right around the leaf. This also makes an attractive gift.

- Use dried creeper, oak, vine and fern leaves to make cards. Fold a rectangle of heavy-duty paper in half to make the card and paste the dried leaves to the front.

- Use gold on white for an elegant look, or combine black and white leaves for a more abstract effect. Remember that you do not have to stick to the more natural colours of leaves – you can use any colour you wish.

The fabric for this tray cloth was decorated with sun technique fabric painting. A thick layer of fabric paint was painted on to the fabric. Then leaves were arranged in the desired positions on the fabric and it was placed outside, in the sun, until the paint had dried. When the leaves were removed, their outlines were etched against the background. The toaster cover was decorated with a row of simple embroidered leaves. Hand-coloured fabric and thread were used here.

Shells

Shells around the house remind us of sand, sea and leisurely, fun-filled days. Their lovely colours and shapes offer many decorative possibilities and a wealth of inspiration for craft motifs.
If you have a supply of real shells, you can use them for a variety of projects, but even without them, you can use the shell theme in your home. Make your own shells using plaster and moulds, or add shell motifs to fabric, wood or glass, using various techniques. Colours do not have to be realistic. White articles with blue shells, for example, create a cool summer feel.
An article that is decorated with shells or shell motifs can be used in any room and is ideal for home-made gifts.

This simple, broad wooden frame was first painted blue to give it a colour-washed look, then decorated with painted plaster shells. Shell motifs were painted on to the hurricane lamp, using glass paint, to make it more interesting.

This wooden 2-litre ice-cream container was first painted neatly and decoupage was then used for shell motifs and an uneven edging strip of gift wrap. By varnishing the container thoroughly, the wood is protected from any dampness the plastic ice-cream container might leave in it. Fabric paint was used to create this place mat featuring shell motifs.

Tips

- Decorate a picture frame with shells. You can use a few shells only, or cover the entire frame with them. Paste the shells in patterns or dot them here and there. You can even make your own frame from driftwood. Put the pieces together roughly, then decorate it with shells.

- Let the children decorate their own bed linen with shell motifs. Measure the area in which they may paint and mark it with masking tape. Allow them to paint shells within the measured strip. This is the ideal project for a rainy day during a beach holiday.

- If you are painting a place mat or tray cloth, make an extra one and keep as a gift for unexpected guests to your holiday home at Christmas time.

- Make curtains or blinds from a plain-coloured fabric and paint a row of shells all around the edge.

- Add shell motifs to candles of various sizes, using paint or decoupage, and group them together to make a pretty focal point.

Line drawings of shells were painted on to this bed linen as decoration. The motifs could also be coloured in, if desired.

Sea

By using sea motifs as decoration on articles, you bring a hint of the sea into your home. Children, in particular, are fond of motifs such as dolphins, seals, octopuses, seahorses and fish, but the theme is by no means restricted to children's rooms. Sea motifs can range from quirky and simple to complex and sophisticated. They are also suitable for various techniques, such as plaster moulds, painting on glass, painting on fabric, appliqué work and decoupage. Although our examples were made mainly in white and shades of blue, any colour can be used to suit your colour scheme.

To decorate this beach bag, motifs were cut from fabric and machine-appliquéd to a hand-painted background. A bought towel is made extra-special by machine-appliquéing whale motifs to the background. The detail was also machine-stitched.

This shelf was lightly colour-washed with white paint and waves were then painted on it. Plaster dolphins, fish and seahorses were painted blue and pasted on to this background. This shelf fits in equally easily in children's rooms or a bathroom. Various sea motifs were painted on the glasses, using glass paint. The glasses can be filled with sand and used as candle holders, or they can be used as drinking glasses. Simple white candles get a new look with plaster ornaments attached to them. Drawing pins can be placed in the plaster ornaments while the plaster is still wet, or the ornaments can be fixed to the candles with wonder putty (Prestik).

Tips

- Paste decorative plaster ornaments directly on to the walls of a room; around the wall switch, for instance.

- Decorate a mirror frame with plaster motifs to suit the theme in the room.

- If fabric containing sea motifs is not available for appliquéing, you can first paint the motifs on to fabric and then appliqué them to the background.

- Paint a glass for each child in the family, using a design of his or her choice.

- Paint sea motifs on to window panes and glass sliding doors using glass paint – preferably the kind that does not need to be baked. Such motifs serve two purposes: as decoration and as a safety precaution.

This wastepaper bin was painted in shades of blue, with the darkest blue at the base, becoming lighter towards the top. Then the background was decorated with decoupage dolphin motifs.

Animals

Farm animals and pets remain popular motifs for decorating articles for the entire house, but mainly the kitchen. Animal motifs are also a fun theme for a child's room. Create a rural atmosphere with subdued, natural colours and motifs, or use bright colours and witty motifs for a playful feel. Appliqué, decoupage, stamps, stencils or painting can be used for the motifs. Use one motif in a room and repeat it on various articles, or use a number of motifs that go together. The possibilities are endless!

The rooster motif for this kitchen wall hanging was painted on fabric and mounted in a rough wooden frame, with chicken wire fronting it instead of glass. An ordinary metal bucket beautifully decorated with a decoupage motif. The background was partially painted before the motif was pasted on to it.

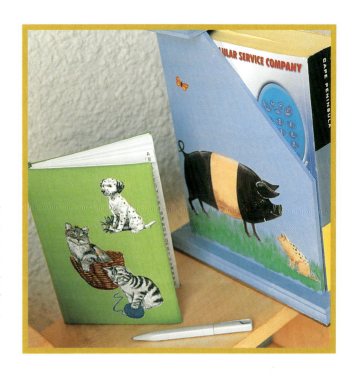

This wooden holder was designed for telephone directories, but is equally suitable for storing recipe books. The holder was first painted neatly with the background colour and the grass was painted with green paint. Decoupage was then used for the motifs. For the notebook, the motifs were appliquéd to the fabric before covering the book. A thin layer of batting was first pasted around the book with transparent glue and the book was then covered with the fabric, in the same way as books are covered with paper.

Tips

- If you have in your kitchen, a small, old cupboard with a rather worn door, you could replace it with a frame containing a fabric-painted motif, such as the rooster wall hanging with chicken wire.

- If you have kitchen cupboards with glass windows, you could mount a fabric-painted picture inside one or more windows. Cut out hardboard the same size as the glass. Paste the picture on to it and fold the raw edges to the back. Place it in the window. Cut another piece of hardboard, about 2 cm larger all round than the previous piece. Place this over the back of the picture and clamp or screw it to the inside of the wooden door frame.

- Make a pretty clock for a kitchen or child's room. Stencil farm animal motifs on to fabric. Mount this in a wooden or embroidered frame and add a clock mechanism.

- Paint a cow motif on to a simple water carafe, using glass paint, and use it as a milk container for the breakfast table.

This wooden egg holder was first colour-washed with paint. Then the decoupage paper motifs were pasted to the wood. Wooden squares with pretty decoupage motifs were used to make the witty coasters.

Flowers

Nothing makes a house prettier or more joyful than a lovely bunch of flowers. Whether it is a large vase of long-stemmed arum lilies or irises or a small pot of brightly coloured pansies, it enhances any room.
Every house needs flowers of some kind or other for decoration. Flowers are just as suitable in a cottage as they are in a modern interior; they can create a joyful, fresh atmosphere or bring a little sunshine into the house during grey winter months. The rich variety of flower types in all colours and shapes is an excellent source of inspiration for motifs. Flower motifs remain ever popular for decorating articles and are suitable for almost any craft form.

The arum lily motif was painted on to this cushion cover with fabric paint. Detail was scratched out on the leaves, using a knitting needle, while the paint was still wet. The leaf and flower motifs were finished off with outliner. The arum lily on the porcelain plate was painted on with glass paint.

Flower motifs were added to the front of this letter holder, using decoupage. The edges were finished off with gold. The wooden tissue box holder was first painted purple to give it a colour-washed look. Then the pansy motifs were painted on the background by hand. The edges were finished off with dark blue and gold.

Tips

- Paint different-coloured pansies on to coffee mugs or cups, using glass paint. Then, when you use them for a special occasion, you can decorate the table or the plate of food with freshly picked pansies from your garden.

- Combine elements from the arum lily motif to use on cushions of different sizes and shapes. For a cylindrical cushion, for example, you could use just one of the arums in the pattern, along with one or two leaves. Group a variety of cushions decorated in this way in a dark corner of a room to liven it up.

- When flowers are scarce and you would like to have some in your home, you can paint a simple flower motif on to an ordinary flower pot, using glass paint. Fill the flower pot with green sprigs, grasses and seeds.

- Fabric articles on to which flowers have been painted look just as good whether the background is painted or left unadorned. Decide for yourself whether you want to paint the background.

- Use the same simple flower motif, pansies for example, as decoration for a tissue box holder and towels for the guest bathroom.

The tablecloth was painted using the flour technique and detail was provided by scratching the motifs, using a knitting needle, while the paint was still wet. Masking tape was used for painting the check pattern in the centre of the tablecloth. A single decoupage flower motif decorates the wooden serviette holder. The edges were finished off in gold.

Topiary trees

Topiary trees of various sizes, shapes and colours are extremely popular among gardeners. Topiary is also a popular theme for crafters and is used as decoration in the home.
The topiary trees do not necessarily have to be in one style. Some look like suckers, others like pyramids or even birds or small animals. You can use green for your design so that it looks natural, or any other colour to match your colour scheme.
Decorate a variety of articles with topiary tree motifs, using any suitable craft technique. Topiary trees as a theme are suitable for any room in the house. The article itself will determine where it can be used.

The topiary tree on the tea cosy was first painted on to the fabric with fabric paint. The detail was embroidered on the cosy, using satin ribbon and embroidery thread. The candles boast decoupage topiary tree motifs. The motifs were first pasted on to the candles and then painted over with a layer of water-based varnish.

This butler's tray was first colour-washed with cream-coloured paint and the edges finished off with green paint. Then decoupage was used to decorate it with various topiary tree motifs, not following any pattern. A simple pillow was transformed into a treasured possession by embroidering topiary tree motifs on it. The buttons for fastening the pillow-case at the front are part of the decoration.

Tips

- Topiary trees are the ideal motif for decorating articles for Christmas time – tray cloths, table-cloths and serviettes, for example.

- Paint topiary trees on to plain-coloured tea cups or coffee mugs with glass paint, to use with the decorated tea cosy. You could also decorate just the sugar bowl and milk jug.

- Paint old bedside cabinets with a light-coloured paint, such as white or cream. Then decorate them with decoupage or painted topiary trees. You can add one tree to the door, or a row of small trees all around the top edge.

- Topiary trees do not have to be green. You can even depict the various seasons with topiary trees, especially by your choice of colours. Use bright green and pink (or any other colour for the flowers) for spring, dark green with fruit for summer, autumn shades for autumn, and a tree without leaves (but still with the right shape) for winter.

- To slot in with the theme, you could even stencil topiary trees on to the wall of the room in which you have topiary tree accessories. A little paint makes a world of difference!

Topiary tree motifs were appliquéd on to these ordinary white towels and cloths as decoration.

Cacti, herbs and lavender

Cacti do not have to be restricted to the garden. Terracotta containers of various sizes, containing succulents, are attractive in any house. In addition, they make the ideal low-maintenance garden for someone who lives in a room or flat. A painted pot plant container holding a cactus is also a good gift. And the unique shape of these plants offers plenty of inspiration for motifs.
White articles decorated with lavender motifs look lovely and make popular presents. Lavender reminds us of France, particularly Provence, with its beautiful lavender fields. Involuntarily, we also think of the fêted French culinary expertise, and of herbs. For this reason, it is not unusual to combine herb and lavender motifs on articles.

These terracotta containers were decorated with cactus motifs, using craft paint.

Tips

- Paint herb motifs on cream-coloured tiles and use them under hot serving dishes.

- Tie string or raffia around a serviette instead of using a serviette ring, and insert a bunch of fresh herbs, to fit in with a herb theme on articles such as place mats and serviettes.

- Decorate an old dinner service which is past its best by painting herbs on it, using glass paint that is baked in an oven.

- If you are having alterations done or building a new house, paint herb, lavender or cactus motifs on to tiles and have them built in in your kitchen. If you want to paint on already built-in tiles, you can paint a coat of varnish over the motif so that it will not wash off easily.

- Embroider lavender motifs on to guest towels and use them with the liquid-soap container.

- Dry lavender and place in a hand-painted mug to decorate a bathroom or bedroom.

- Paint herb, cactus or lavender motifs on to cards and keep them for when you need cards for a birthday or other occasion.

An ordinary liquid-soap container is transformed by a piece of fabric, embroidered with lavender motifs and fastened with Velcro strips at the ends. When the soap container is empty, the fabric can be fitted around the new container. Lavender sprigs were embroidered on to coarsely woven fabric to decorate the potpourri bag. A simple lavender motif, painted on to the white porcelain mug with glass paint, makes it special.

These unique place mats were created by embroidering simple herb motifs on to bought place mats. The herb motifs on the serviettes were painted with fabric paint.

Vegetables

With the current emphasis on eating fresh vegetables for a healthy body, vegetables are good news! Never before have vegetable motifs been as popular as they are now. The variety of kinds, shapes and colours provide excellent inspiration for motifs.
The vegetable theme is particularly suited to the kitchen, but can also work well in an informal dining room or braai area. Choose a single vegetable theme; or use a colour theme.

Vegetable motifs were hand-painted on to this wooden bread bin, after it had been neatly painted in green.

A bought place mat was decorated by appliquéing a brightly coloured pumpkin motif on to it. Glass paint was used to paint the carrot motif all around the rim of the porcelain plate.

Tips

- Paint various vegetable motifs on to an ordinary white dinner service. You can use just one motif on each article, or a variety of motifs.

- White or cream-coloured articles decorated with a single cabbage motif are very popular and they can look very smart. Combine articles bearing cabbage motifs to make a small display in your kitchen or dining room. Antique porcelain with this theme would also be effective in a display.

- Paint vegetable motifs on tiles with glass paint and have them mounted against the wall. Or mount the tiles in attractive wooden frames, without glass, and use them to decorate your kitchen.

- Make a place mat and serviette for each family member, bearing their own vegetable motif.

- Renew old, worn-out kitchen cupboards by painting them neatly and then adding vegetable motifs to the doors.

This versatile cutlery holder can also be used as a salad dressing holder or as storage for all the large serving spoons and ladles used in the kitchen. The holder was colour-washed with cream-coloured paint and decorated with decoupage. To finish, the edges were painted dark green. The garlic-bread holder was first given a two-colour-washed effect, then the appropriate garlic motif was painted inside.

An ordinary kitchen dishcloth gets a different look with an appliquéd red chilli motif.

Fruit

When we think of ripe, juicy fruit, we also inevitably think of summer, sun and having fun. Fruit has been a decorating theme for centuries, and remains popular. This theme does not have to be restricted to the kitchen. You can use one fruit as a theme and repeat the motif, or combine a variety of fruits and motifs. The motifs can be of whole, halved or sliced fruit. You can experiment with various techniques and choose shades of colour to suit your colour scheme.

This functional wooden container was specially made to hold a 5-litre juice or wine box. It was decorated with decoupage. The old tray was bought at a flea market. It was sanded before decoupage was used for the fruit design. Extra lines and curls were added to the decoupage design, using a black permanent (indelible) pen, before the podge was painted over.

Decoupage lemon motifs were added to this key rack after it had been neatly painted. A gold rim finishes off the article.

Tips

- Keep a lookout at flea markets for articles that you can use to decorate with motifs.

- Let your children paint their own designs on a 5-litre wooden container for juice or wine, and write their names on it. This will make an unusual gift for any father, and is the ideal project for Father's Day.

- Fruit designs are pretty on hand-painted tablecloths. Use one fruit as a motif and repeat it, or paint a variety of fruits on the tablecloth.

- Cushions displaying fruit motifs look attractive on dining-room chairs and in the sitting room. Paint the motifs with fabric paint, or appliqué or embroider them.

- Make your own embroidery canvas projects by painting some of the motifs on to embroidery canvas. Use the right colours of thread and embroider the motif.

The serviette holder was first painted to give it a colour-washed look, then the lemon motifs were painted on it. The smaller motifs at the top of the container are repeats of parts of the large motif on the side. The watermelon motif that decorates the bought cookie jar was painted on with glass paint.

Motifs

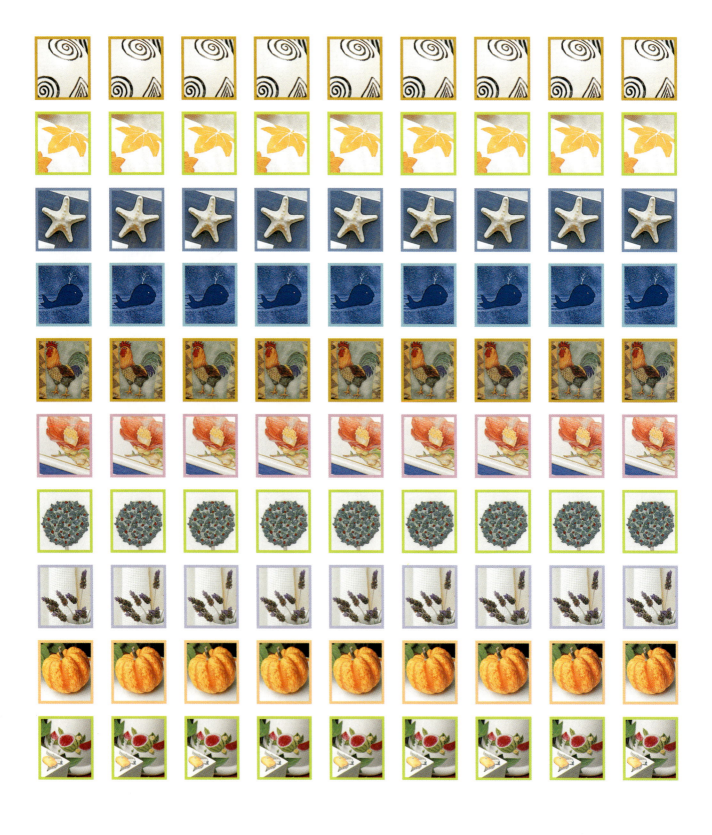

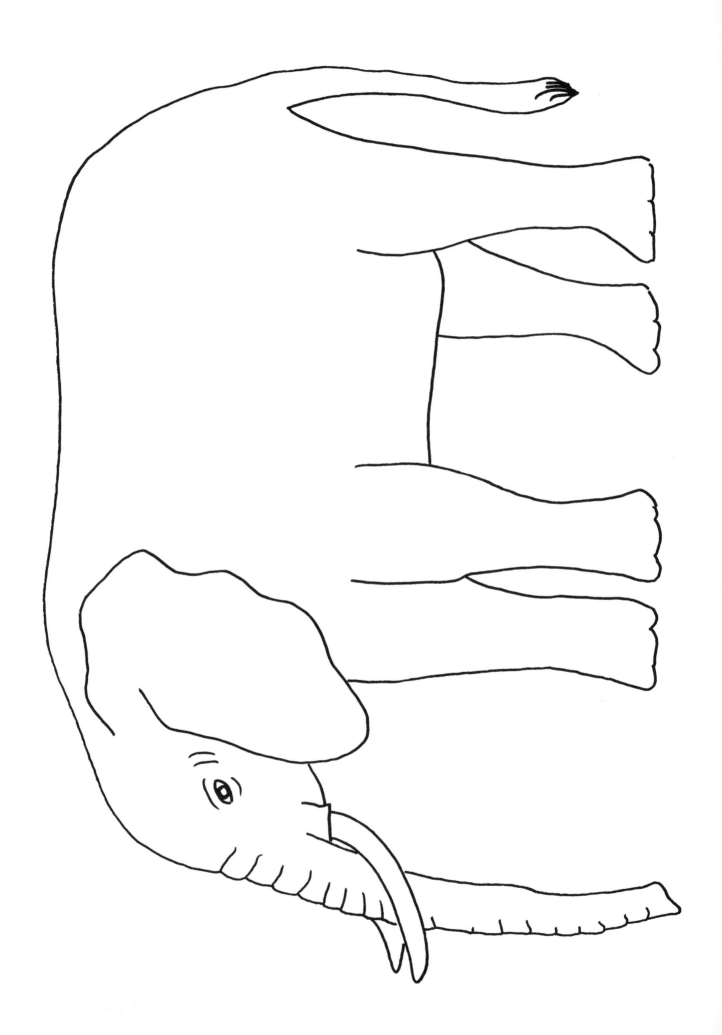

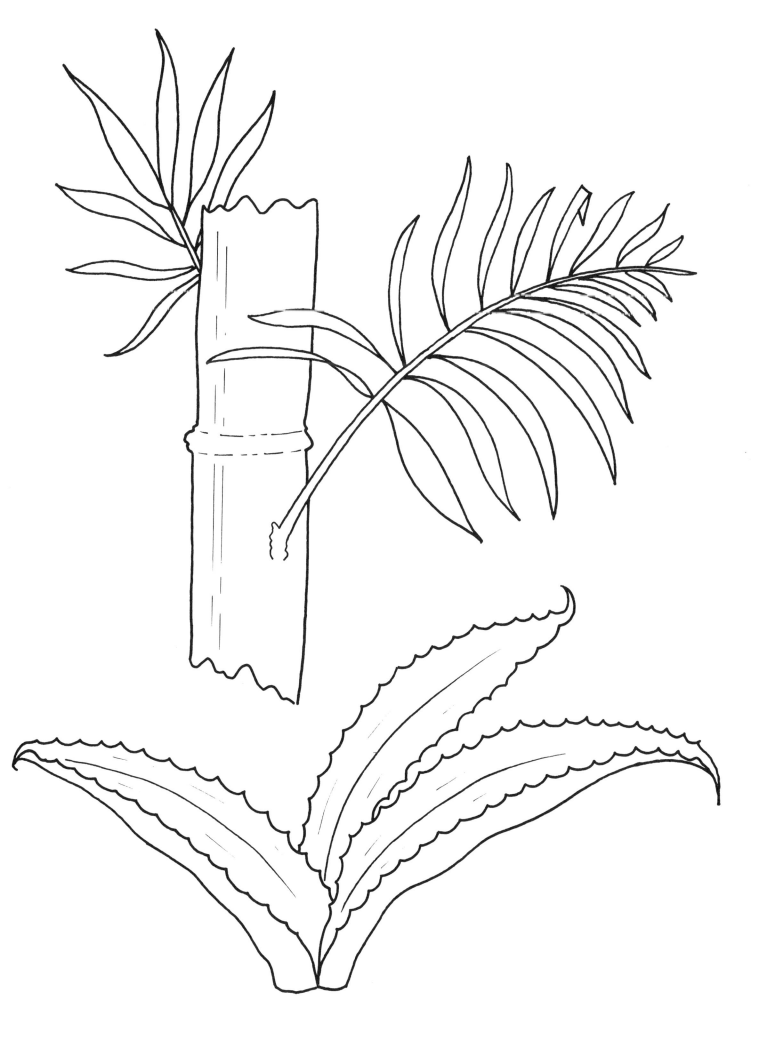

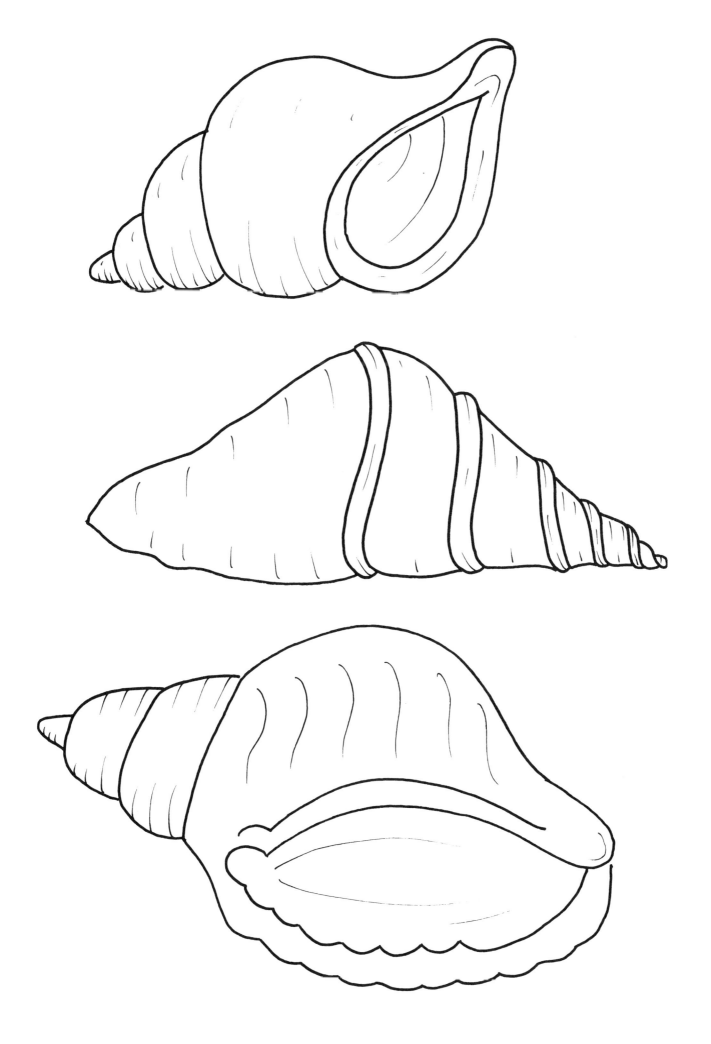

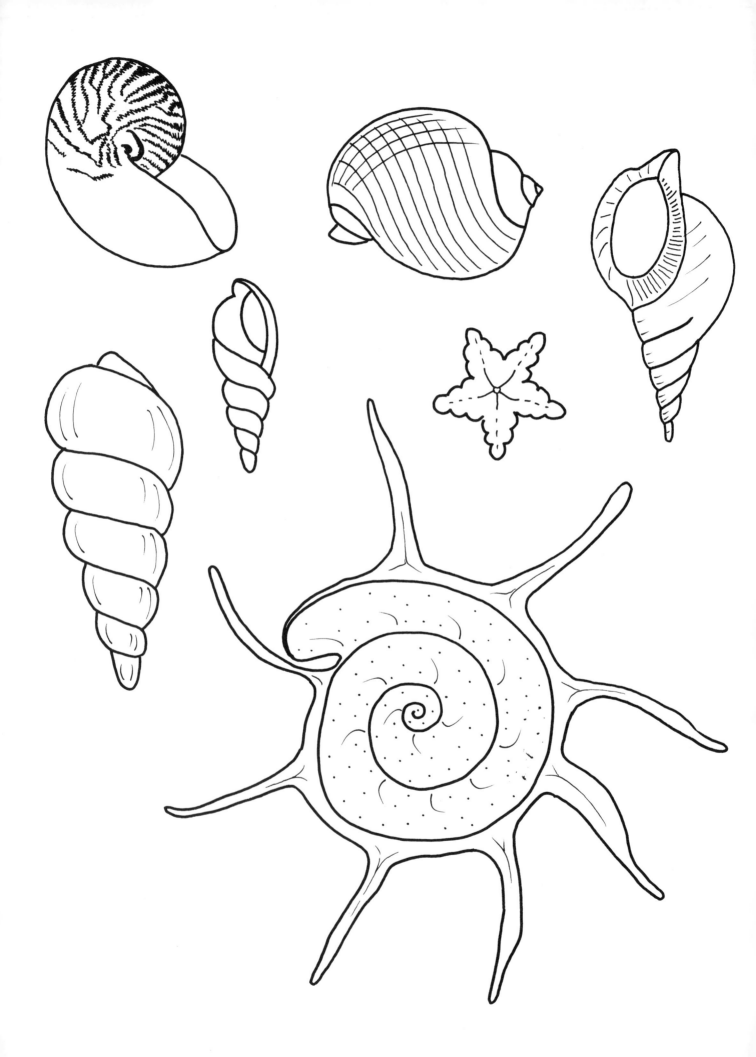

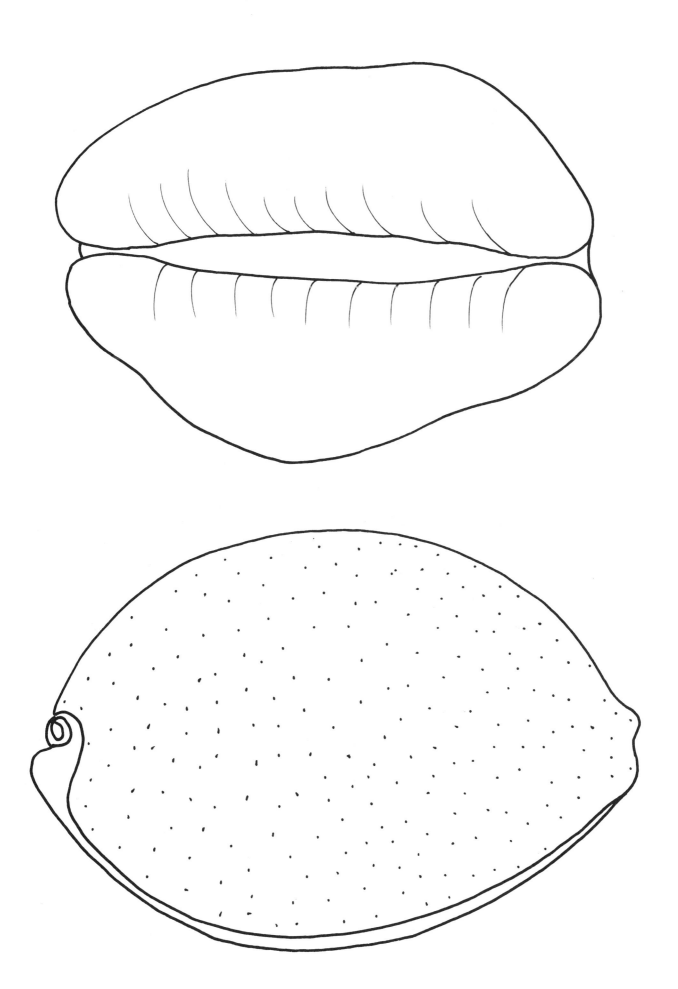

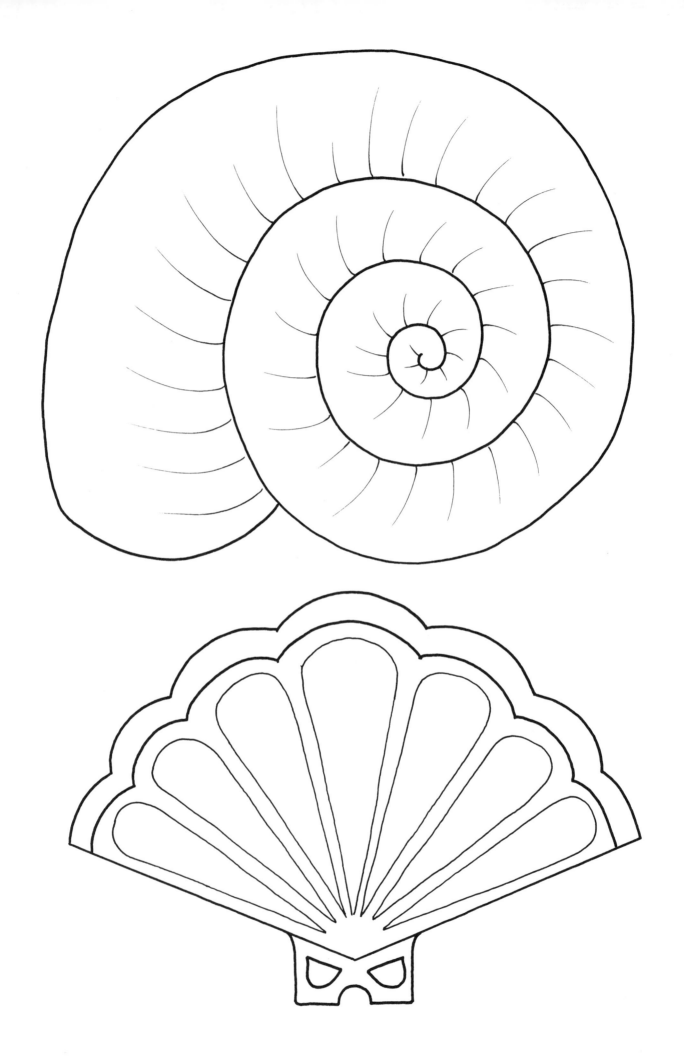

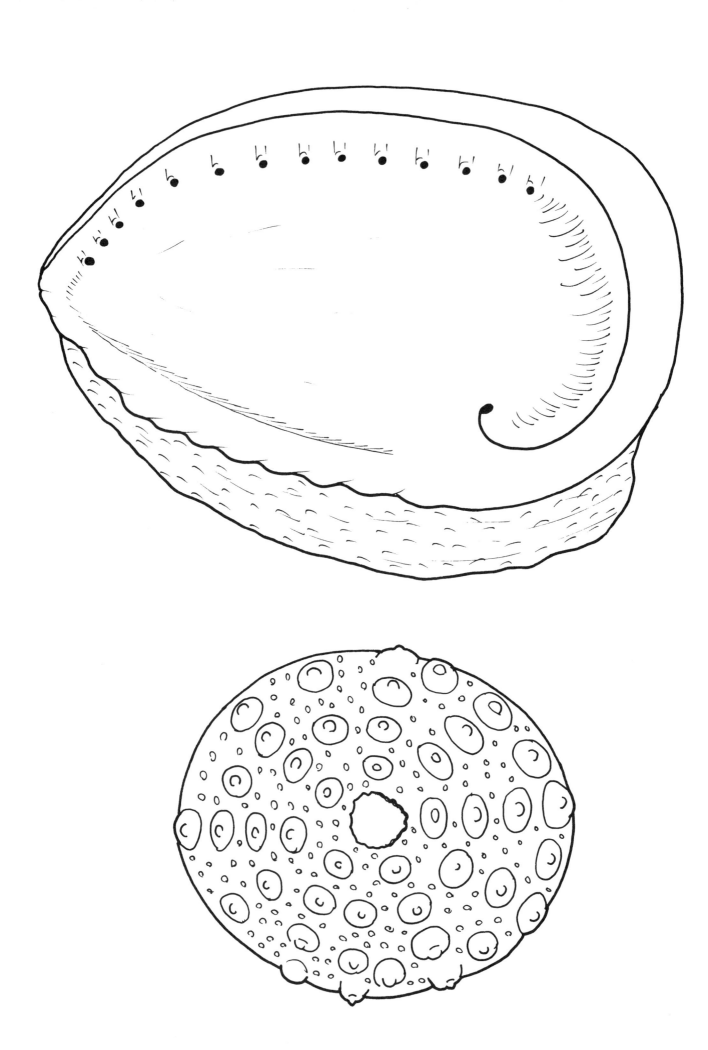

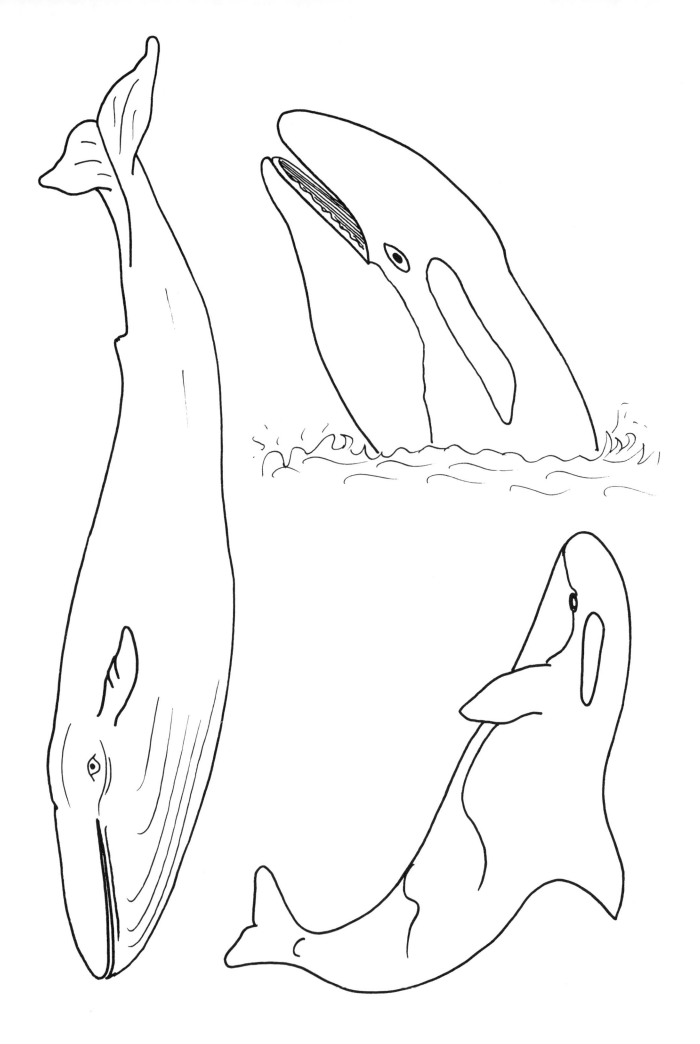

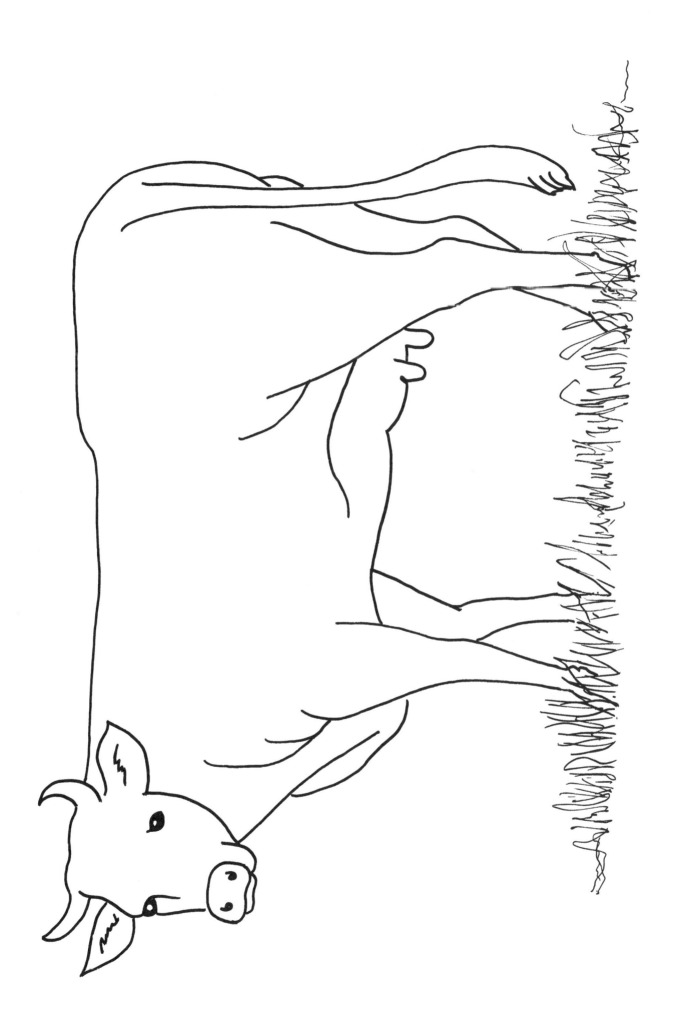

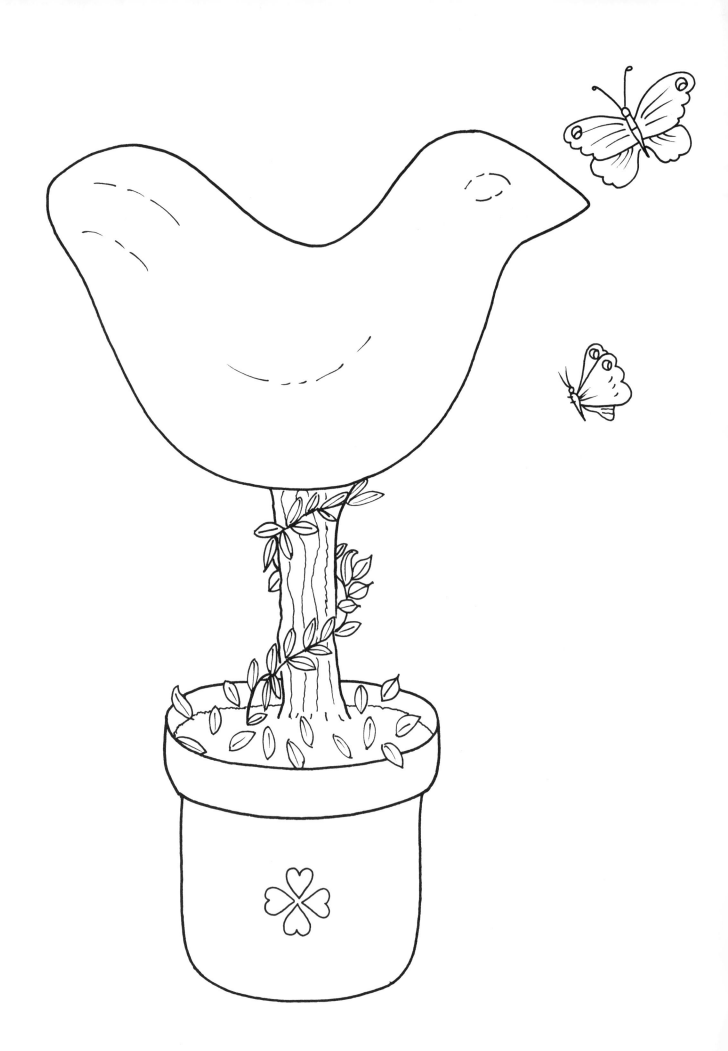

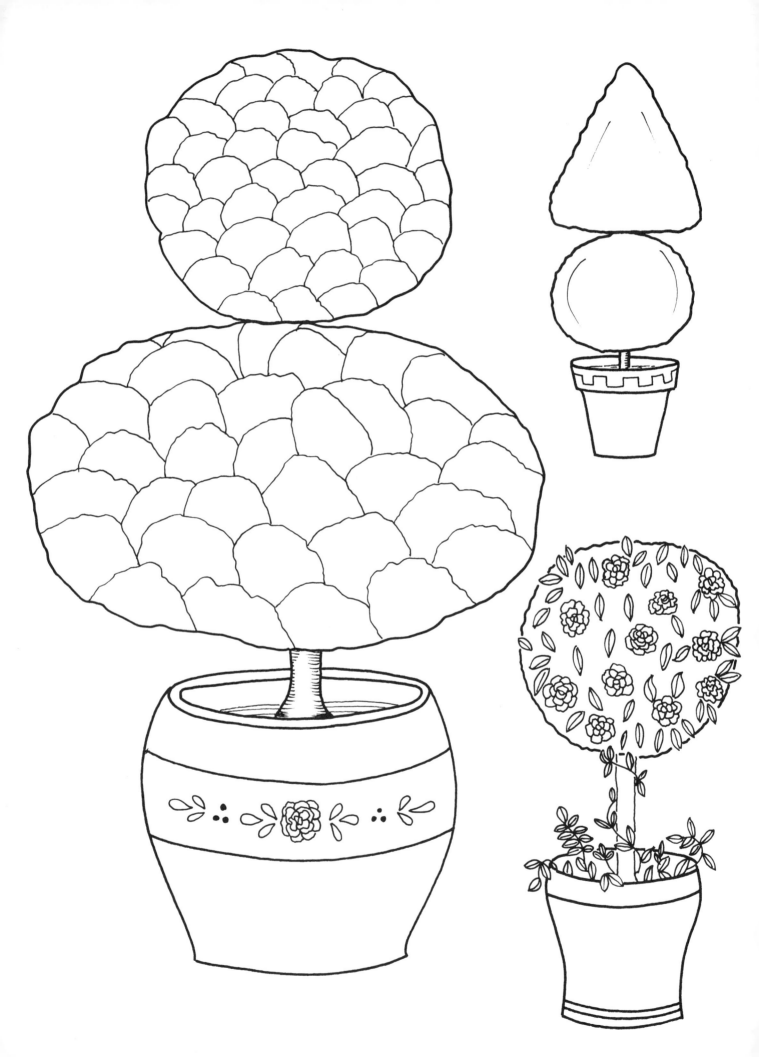

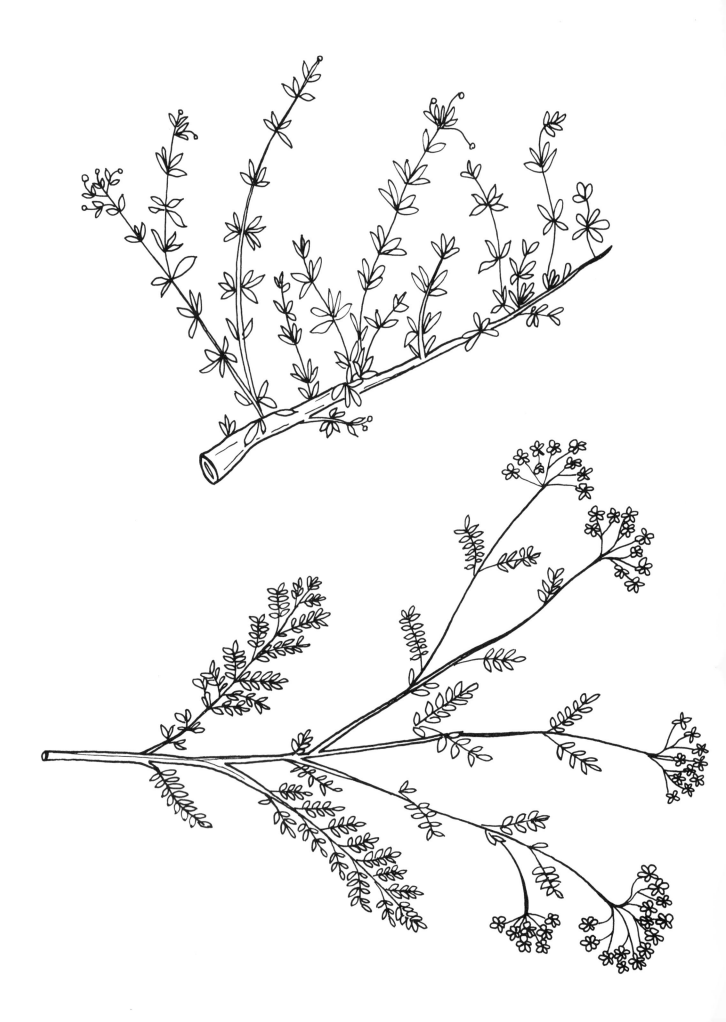

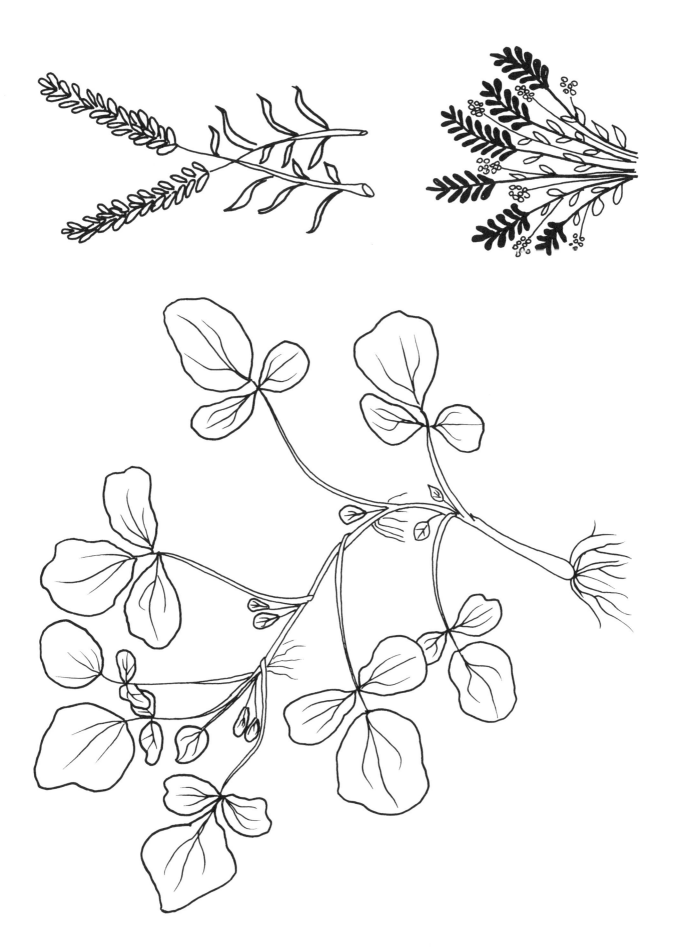

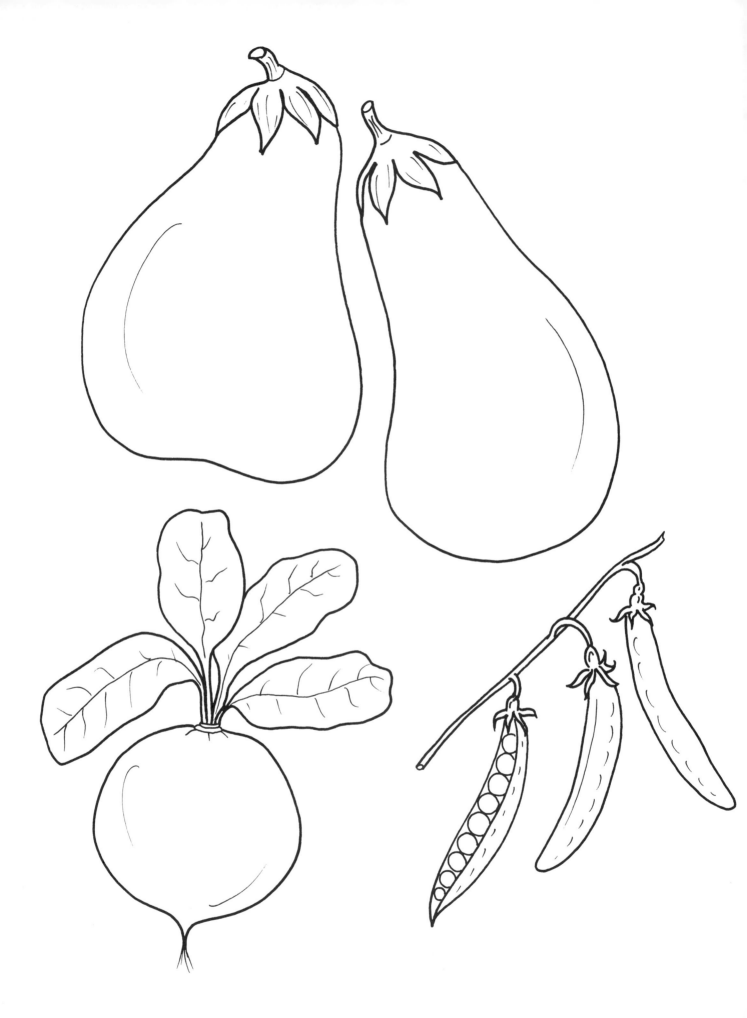

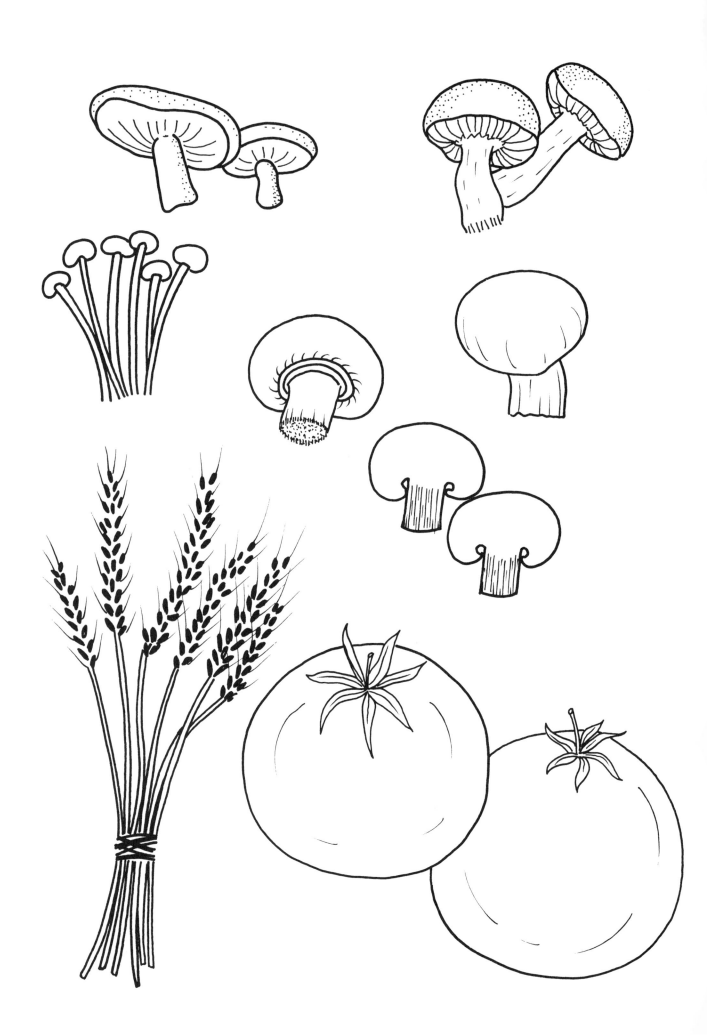

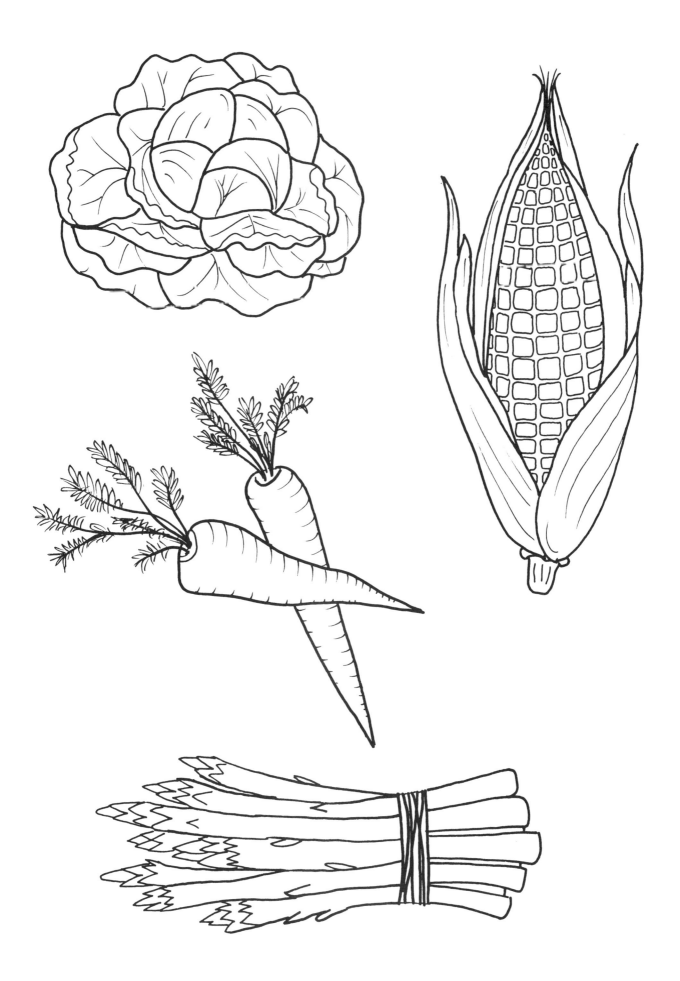

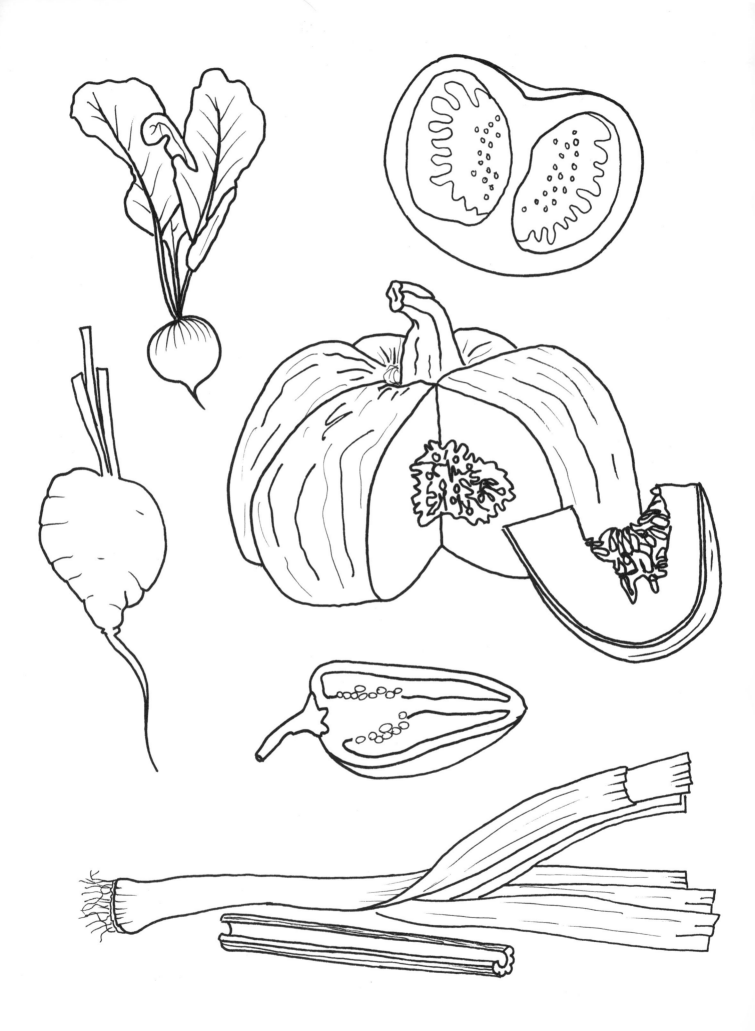

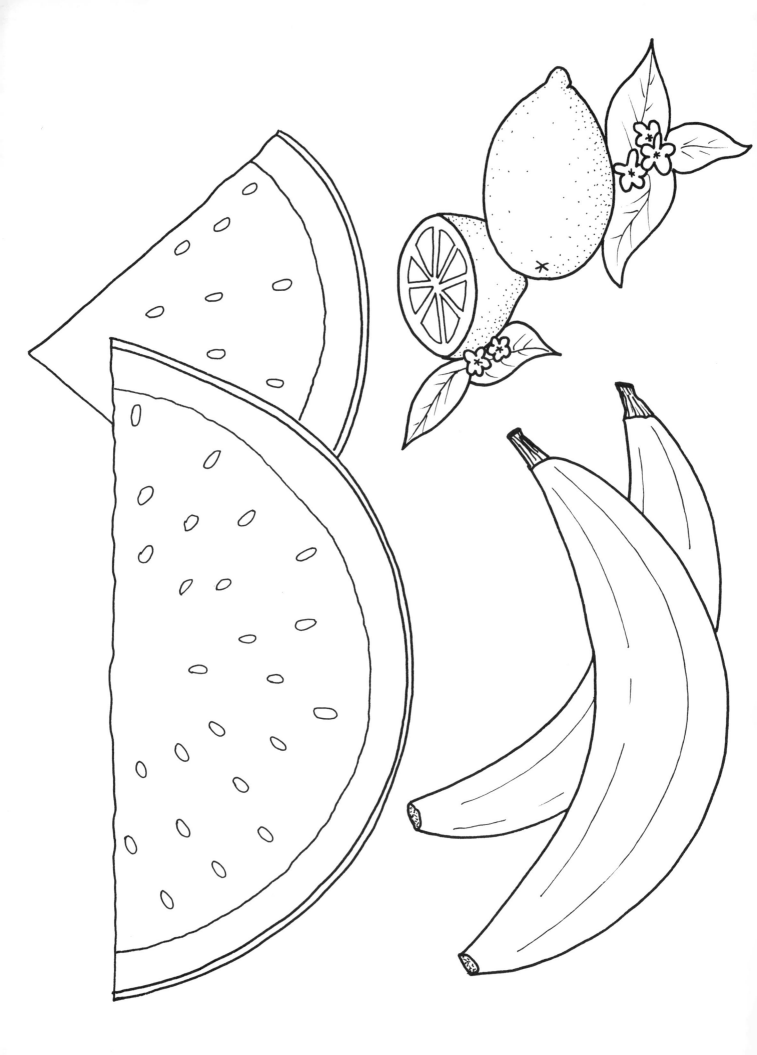

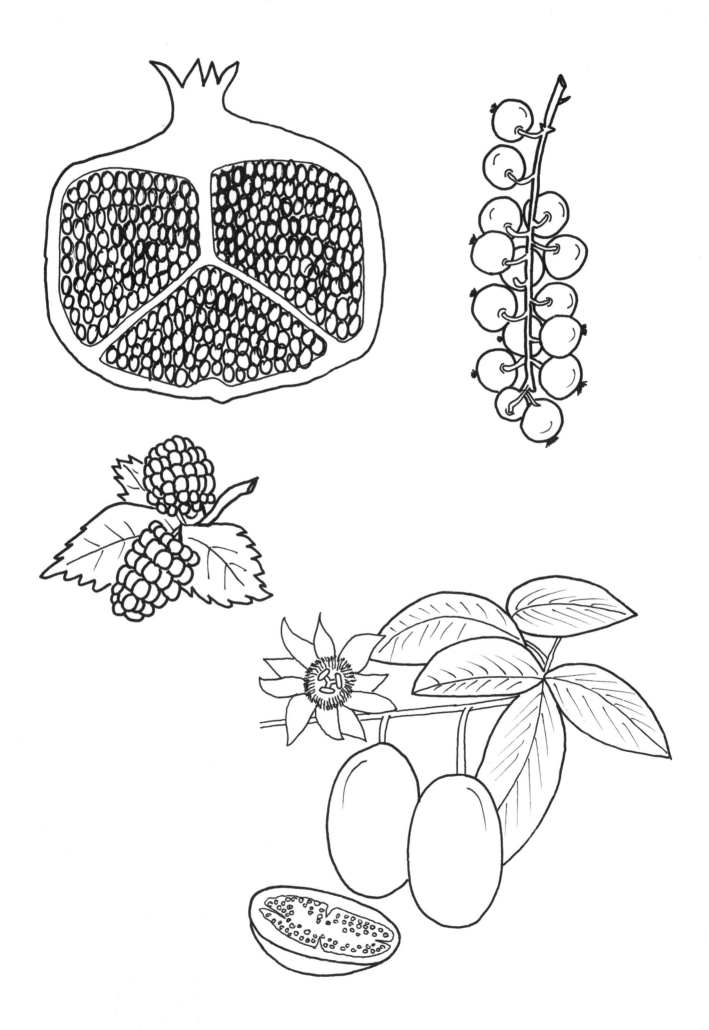

24SEVEN issue 3
MAKING SENSE OF YOUR ISSUES

Allison Bond

© 2003 Folens Limited on behalf of the author.

United Kingdom: Folens Publishers, Apex Business Centre, Boscombe Road, Dunstable, LU5 4RL.
Email: folens@folens.com

Ireland: Folens Publishers, Greenhills Road, Tallaght, Dublin 24.
Email: info@folens.ie

Poland: JUKA, ul. Renesansowa 38, Warsaw 01-905.

Folens publications are protected by international copyright laws. All rights are reserved. The copyright of all materials in this publication, except where otherwise stated, remains the property of the publisher and author. No part of this publication may be reproduced, stored in a retrieval system, or transmitted, in any form or by any means, for whatever purpose, without the written permission of Folens Limited.

Folens allows photocopying of pages marked 'copiable page' for educational use, providing that this use is within the confines of the purchasing institution. Copiable pages should not be declared in any return in respect of any photocopying licence.

Allison Bond hereby asserts her moral right to be identified as the author of this work in accordance with the Copyright, Designs and Patents Act 1988.

Editor: Melody Ismail
Layout artist: Tech-Set Ltd.
Cover design: Martin Cross

First published in 2003 by Folens Limited.

Every effort has been made to contact copyright holders of material used in this publication. If any copyright holder has been overlooked, we should be pleased to make any necessary arrangements.

British Library Cataloguing in Publication Data. A catalogue record for this publication is available from the British Library.

ISBN 1 84303 309 7

Contents

Series Overview & Introduction 4
How 24SEVEN links with the programmes of study for Citizenship and PSHE 5

What's On Your Mind?
Dear diary 6
Email emergency 7
Backgrounds 8
P@rty time! 9
A Dad for a fortnight 10
Sex education at school 11
To have or not to have – that is the question 12
The thin blue line 13
Be wise to STIs 14

The Main Event
What are they like? 15
Diamond 9 – what's important in a school? 16
Star schools 17
Where to next? & The law says 18
Student exclusions 19
Different for girls? 20
Poverty – just an excuse? 21
Hiding in the headlines 22
Looking back – a teacher speaks out 23
DIY education 24

Friendship
Meet my mates 25
Gossip at the garage 26
Not all bad news 27
Phone up for a little friendly advice 28
A bridge too far 29
Doer or doormat? 30
Magic mates & Friends 4 ever? 31
Focus v friendship: Emma's story 32

Series Overview

Having introduced Citizenship and PSHE to the curriculum, the Secretary of State for Education has recognised that education needs to involve making life skills and everyday choices an integral part of students' education. My aim in creating 24SEVEN is to provide 11–14 year olds with relevant and engaging starting points for the development of this knowledge.

Followed as a complete course, 24SEVEN will give you effective coverage of Citizenship and PSHE at KS3. Issues 1 and 2 are targeted at Year 7 students, Issues 3 and 4 at Year 8 students and Issues 5 and 6 at Year 9 students. Each theme will provide you with at least half a term's work. However, since the themes themselves are broken down into smaller spreads, you may like to use these to support and supplement your existing resources. 24SEVEN is not a course that needs to be followed slavishly.

Use of the material is very flexible. Topics can be explored thematically or used in a more 'pick and mix' fashion. However, like all resources, 24SEVEN must be used with sensitivity and consideration. Some topics may not be appropriate for the particular group you are teaching: whereas some topics may have a particular resonance with your school. You know your class and it has to be your call.

The student material opens up a number of issues and is designed to be chatty and informative – a good read in itself, not a lecture. This series encourages young people to consider and share their ideas about some challenging and potentially embarrassing scenarios. Students are encouraged to think through difficult situations and to consider the long-term consequences of their decisions or their actions.

The follow-on activities in the teachers' notes encourage students to challenge, consider, question and research in order to gain a deeper understanding of the issues being covered. Many problems are inter-related and students will be encouraged to think about how difficulties in one area of life impact on other areas. 24SEVEN operates in their world and students need to think and talk about what matters to them. Students are actively encouraged to voice their opinions, but they must always be prepared to justify their point of view. The use of italics in the teachers' notes shows where you address the class, the non-italicised text gives you direct instructions.

As a practising teacher, I always find it useful to establish a few ground rules for discussion work along the lines of 'I'm going to make sure that everyone gets a chance to say something today'. This ensures that everyone knows what is expected of them. Once the thinking and talking activities are finished, students can commit their ideas to paper.

You will need to make a judicious selection from the follow-on activities. The subject matter – being topical – is unpredictable. Some activities may take ten minutes, whilst others, if they are to be covered effectively, will take an entire lesson. The follow-on activities give you both flexibility and choice. However you use 24SEVEN, you can look forward to lively, topical and relevant exchanges with your students.

Allison Bond

Issue 3 Introduction

It is important to look, at an early stage, at sex and sexual health as students often develop intense relationships at a young age. This is dealt with by the theme *What's On Your Mind?* 24SEVEN takes a candid look at the implications of sex and the possible consequences of unplanned and unprotected sex. It does not presuppose that all Year 8 students are sexually active. However, 24SEVEN addresses students' need to know the truth about a delicate subject about which they often receive only edited highlights.

Why do school and education matter? Who are schools for? Are they working? Could they do better? These are just some of the ideas explored in the section on education – *The Main Event*. Education cannot right all wrongs, but it can make a difference. These topics set out to explore the positive aspects of education. Work covered here forms a platform for work on careers in Issue 6 – *Which Way?*

Schools would not be the same without school friends going through stages of breaking up and making up. The *Friendship* theme looks at the positive and negative effects of friendships, why some friendships work and why others fail.

How 24SEVEN links with the programmes of study for Citizenship and PSHE

24SEVEN Theme: What's On Your Mind?

Citizenship

Developing skills of enquiry and communication.

2. Pupils should be taught to:

   a. think about topical political, spiritual, moral, social and cultural issues, problems and events by analysing information and its sources, including ICT-based sources

   c. contribute to group and exploratory class discussions and take part in debate.

PSHE

Developing a healthy, safer lifestyle.

2. Pupils should be taught:

   a. to recognise the physical and emotional changes that take place at puberty and how to manage these changes in a positive way

   e. in a context of the importance of relationships, about human reproduction, contraception, sexually transmitted infections, HIV and high-risk behaviours including early sexual activity.

24SEVEN Theme: The Main Event

PSHE

Developing confidence and responsibility and making the most of their abilities

1. Pupils should be taught:

   a. to reflect on and assess their strengths in relation to personality, work and leisure.

24SEVEN Theme: Friendship

PSHE

Developing confidence and responsibility and making the most of their abilities.

1. Pupils should be taught:

   c. to recognise how others see them and be able to give and receive constructive feedback and praise.

Developing good relationships and respecting the differences between people.

3. Pupils should be taught:

   c. about the nature of friendship and how to make and keep friends

   h. to recognise that goodwill is essential to positive and constructive relationships

   i. to negotiate within relationships, recognising that actions have consequences, and when and how to make compromises.

24SEVEN

Teachers' Notes

Theme: What's On Your Mind?

Topic: Dear diary

Student Reference: Issue 3, pages 4-5

C/PSHE Link: Citizenship 2a, 2c; PSHE 2a, 2e

Objective: To introduce the importance of safe and reliable contraception. To introduce the family problems that may be caused by under-age sexual activity.

Follow-on

1. Read the 'Dear diary' spread. To what extent do you think the people in this situation are behaving responsibly? What risks are the mother, the boyfriend and the girl taking?

2. The mother says that the girl is too young to get so involved. If you were the parent in this situation, what would you think? What would you say to your daughter?

3. If the girl in this story devotes herself at this age to her boyfriend, can you think of some difficulties she may face when she gets older?

4. In pairs, improvise a scene between the mother and the daughter when the daughter first brings up the idea of going on the pill. Students may need starting points to get them underway.

   Opening lines for person role playing mum:
   - 'I never did like that boy. I knew he'd be trouble the minute I set eyes on him.'
   - 'You are too young to know what you're doing. The only form of contraception you need to think about using is the word "No".'
   - 'It's all those magazines you've been reading – they're just full of sex and they've given you stupid ideas.'

   Opening lines for person role playing girl:
   - 'Mum, you know that me and Gary are really serious about each other.'
   - 'Do you remember Trish from my class? She brought her baby into school today to talk about what it's like being a teenage mum.'
   - 'Suppose you really wanted to show someone that you loved them, Mum, what would you do?'

5. From your local community, collect a range of information about contraception. Find out about how it works, its reliability, what might prevent it working effectively and any possible side effects or risks to health. Collect these to form a project or information pack and make them available for other students who want to find out more.

6. Students could be asked to debate one of the following motions:
   - The age of consent should be lowered to 14 years of age.
   - Contraceptives should be available to those aged under 16, without their parents' knowledge or consent.

24SEVEN

Teachers' Notes

Theme: What's On Your Mind?

Topic: Email emergency

Student Reference: Issue 3, page 7

C/PSHE Link: Citizenship 2a, 2c; PSHE 2a, 2e

Objective: To provide an opportunity for students to find out about the safety and effectiveness of various forms of contraception.

NB Effective sex education and discussions of sex with young people often have the best results when discussed within the framework of a relationship – and the variety of definitions that 'relationship' raises. It is advisable to spend two or three consecutive lessons on this work.

Follow-on

1. *Make use of the school library, biology department, magazines, the Internet and resources from health centres to compile an A4 fact sheet on four different methods of contraception. Your fact sheet must include the following details:*

   - *name of the method*
   - *how it works*
   - *how reliable it is*
   - *possible side effects or long-term health risks.*

   Illustrations and quotes from health experts and newspaper stories will help to bring dry facts to life. If appropriate, make the finished fact sheets available in school.

2. Provide students with a photocopy of the sheet on the following page. *People use different forms of contraception for a number of reasons. The nature of the relationship between a couple, and their religious and cultural beliefs will all influence the choice of contraception. Read through the different scenarios given on the 'Backgrounds' sheet and, casting yourself in the role of an expert, decide which method of contraception – if any – you would advise. You may choose to offer advice rather than recommend contraception.*

Backgrounds

Read the background to each case below and write down the advice you would give to those involved. Would you recommend contraception? If so, which method? You must give a reason for your recommendation.

Background

A 15-year-old boy is encouraged by a 17-year-old girl, who he does not know very well, to have sex with her.

Advice/Method of contraception ....

....

Reason ....

Background

A 15-year-old boy and girl in a relationship have decided to have sex but do not want the girl to get pregnant.

Advice/Method of contraception ....

....

Reason ....

Background

A 15-year-old girl who is being pressured into having sex by her 16-year-old boyfriend.

Advice/Method of contraception ....

....

Reason ....

Background

A 17-year-old girl in a stable relationship, who suffers from bulimia.

Advice/Method of contraception ....

....

Reason ....

Background

A newly married Catholic couple who do not want to have children for at least three years.

Advice/Method of contraception ....

....

Reason ....

Background

A married couple who have three children; neither wants any more.

Advice/Method of contraception ....

....

Reason ....

24SEVEN

Teachers' Notes

Theme: What's On Your Mind?

Topic: P@rty time!

Student Reference: Issue 3, pages 8–9

C/PSHE Link: Citizenship 2a, 2c; PSHE 2a, 2e

Objective: To explore the issues of high-risk sexual behaviour, early sexual activity and sexually transmitted diseases.

Follow-on

1. The 'P@rty time!' spread shows how, even before he got to the party, Mike felt under pressure to change his behaviour. Can you explain why?

2. At the party, Mike didn't behave as he usually would. Who or what influenced him there? How?

3. Who or what may have influenced Jenny to behave in the way that she did?

4. Mike, Will and Jenny all share a certain amount of responsibility for what happened at the party. Working in groups, decide on a number to represent each person's level of responsibility as a percentage. Compare and contrast your findings with those of other groups.

5. Mike is now terrified about the consequences of his actions. If you were to offer him advice as to what he should do now, what would it be?

6. Imagine Mike, five years older, talking to a group of young people about his first experiences of sex. What sort of things might he make comments about? How do you think he will look back at the event? Will the memories be positive or negative? Write an account of what he would say as a feature article for 24SEVEN, using no more than 150 words.

7. Does a girl who 'sleeps around', get a worse reputation than a boy would? Explain your answer.

8. How does a person recover their reputation after an incident like this?

24SEVEN

Teachers' Notes

Theme: What's On Your Mind?

Topic: A Dad for a fortnight

Student Reference: Issue 3, pages 10-11

C/PSHE Link: Citizenship 2a, 2c; PSHE 2a, 2e

Objective: To explore the loss of freedom associated with parenthood.

Follow-on

1. Read the 'A Dad for a fortnight' spread. If you had an egg to look after for 14 days and nights, what sorts of thing would you have to give up? Compile a list and share your ideas with a partner or discuss in a small group.

2. Do you think that boys and girls of your age would miss out on the same kinds of thing? What would be some of the similarities or some of the differences? Would things be different if the spread was about being a mum for a fortnight?

3. Take a moment to imagine that the egg is totally dependent on you for its safety and survival. What are some of the positive feelings you might have towards it? Try to come up with five or six. The first positive feeling may be something basic such as, 'I like my egg. It's a nice colour and shape.'

4. Would your feelings grow stronger if you looked after the egg for longer?

5. Can you think of some of the negative feelings that you might have towards the egg when it begins to interfere with your everyday life? Again, see if you can think of five or six. One example might be: 'I might feel jealous of my friends who don't have the same responsibilities as me.'

6. To a certain extent, this experiment has limitations, for example, the egg does not need feeding or entertaining, like a baby does. What are the additional responsibilities that would have to be taken on when caring for a baby?

7. How do you think that the boy in the spread probably treated girls before his surprising 'eggsperience'? How do you think that he will treat them now? To record your ideas, divide a piece of paper in half and head one half 'BEFORE' and the other half 'AFTER'. Be prepared to share your ideas with others in the class.

8. The purpose of the egg experiment was not to dissuade people from ever becoming parents. What do you think that it was for? Compile a list of your suggestions.

9. Do you think the experiment was effective? If so, why?

24SEVEN

Teachers' Notes

Theme: What's On Your Mind?

Topic: Sex education at school

Student Reference: Issue 3, pages 12-13

C/PSHE Link: Citizenship 2a, 2c; PSHE 2a, 2e

Objective: To introduce the difficulties of teaching sex education in schools. To introduce the prospect of negotiated learning of a potentially embarrassing subject.

Follow-on

1. Read the comments made by the teaching staff in the 'Sex education at school' spread. Working in pairs, compile a list of the advantages and disadvantages of each member of staff's approach to the subject of sex education. These can then be collated on the board as a starting point.

2. How do you think sex education should be taught? Should you be encouraged to talk about sex at a much younger age? Should sex education not be available at all?

3. Again in pairs, decide which member of staff you think that you would learn most from. Who would you learn least from, and why? Who might give you the most accurate, up-to-date and impartial advice? Report back your decision to the class and see if there is agreement or disagreement.

4. Talking about sex in school can cause a great deal of embarrassment for teachers and students. Can you think why?

5. Some parents are worried about what their children may be taught during sex education lessons. Imagine you are a parent: think of five things you may be concerned about your child knowing. Why would you have these concerns?

6. As a class, compile a list of five ground rules to try to make talking about sex a little less embarrassing. Design an A5- or A4-sized poster displaying these rules.

7. Your teachers can only cover a limited amount of sex education with you. If you wanted to find out more from sources that give you accurate and impartial advice, where would you go? Make a note of these possible options.

© Folens (copiable page)

24SEVEN

Teachers' Notes

Theme: What's On Your Mind?

Topic: To have or not to have – that is the question

Student Reference: Issue 3, pages 14-15

C/PSHE Link: Citizenship 2a, 2c; PSHE 2a, 2e

Objective: To discuss the reasons that lay behind early sexual activity. To look at the arguments for delaying sexual activity.

Follow-on

1. Can you think of any reasons, in addition to those on the 'To have or not to have …' spread, why people are having sex under age?

2. What reasons do young people give who are choosing to delay having sex?

3. Are the reasons either for having sex or for delaying sex the same for young men and young women? In groups of no more than four, go through the reasons previously given and discuss whether or not they are specific to one gender.

4. In groups, choose four statements from each set of responses on the 'To have or not to have …' spread. Do you agree or disagree with that person's point of view? What does the person's opinion tell you either about that individual's character or that individual's attitude to under-age sex?

Ask students to set out their answers using the following template.

Looking at attitudes to sex		
Statement	**Agree (✓) or Disagree (X)**	**Character/Attitude**
People seemed to like me more if I did it with them.	X	Not much self-esteem or idea of what real friends are. They don't see sex with somebody as special or important.

5. Some high-profile media stars make very public announcements about preserving their virginity. Would their attitude influence young people? Do you think it could be a ploy for extra publicity? Explain your point of view.

6. "The fashion industry encourages young children to dress like their idols, often in a provocative manner which can promote early sexual activity. The industry should therefore be regulated by concerned adults." What are your opinions on this statement? Who should the adults involved be?

24SEVEN

Teachers' Notes

Theme: What's On Your Mind?

Topic: The thin blue line

Student Reference: Issue 3, pages 16-17

C/PSHE Link: Citizenship 2a, 2c; PSHE 2a, 2e

Objective: To look at the long-term consequences of unplanned pregnancy.

Follow-on

1. Since you are all below the age of consent, do you think you should be considering the dilemmas faced by the girl in 'The thin blue line' spread? Justify your point of view.

2. What is your reaction to each of the options suggested on the spread? Have you read anything that surprises or shocks you? Has the spread highlighted anything that, up to now, you had not thought about?

3. How would you feel about each of these options if you were either the girl or the father of the baby?

4. Where in your local area can you find accurate and reliable information about the issues of adoption, early parenthood and abortion? How would you find out such information? Who would you go to for help and advice?

5. Imagine the girl from the spread comes to you for advice. What would your advice to her be? Write her an email, of up to 200 words, explaining to her why you think she should follow one particular course of action.

6. Find out what rights adopted children have. Are they legally entitled to know their parents' names? Can they trace their birth parents?

7. Find out what rights a mother has who has given her baby up for adoption. Is she able to contact the child at a later date? Is she allowed to send birthday cards? Does the natural father have any rights?

24SEVEN

Teachers' Notes

Theme: What's On Your Mind?

Topic: Be wise to STIs

Student Reference: Issue 3, pages 18–19

C/PSHE Link: Citizenship 2a, 2c; PSHE 2a, 2e

Objective: To encourage students to research and present their findings about sexually transmitted diseases.

NB In order to get the best results from the activities, this subject matter should be worked on over a number of lessons.

Follow-on

1. In groups, prepare a three-minute news bulletin, which aims to explore the link between early, or increased, sexual activity and the rise in sexually transmitted infections (STIs). Your preparation must include the following:

   - a script for the reporter or interviewer to link the bulletin together
   - a medical opinion from an expert
   - an opinion from a man or woman on the street
   - an opinion from a young person, perhaps at a disco or party.

   Your interview will be better if you complete some background research on STIs before you start. If these take shape effectively, you may like to use props, costumes and a stage set and go on to video the extract as a resource for other students.

2. If appropriate, you could ask the students to find out about some or all of the STIs mentioned in the 'Be wise to STIs' spread. Students can record their findings in a table using the headings shown below.

STI Name	Symptoms	Treatment

24SEVEN

Teachers' Notes

Theme: The Main Event

Topic: What are they like?

Student Reference: Issue 3, pages 20-21

C/PSHE Link: PSHE 1a; Citizenship scheme of work, KS3, Unit 14

Objective: To provide the opportunity for students to talk about their experiences of school. To give students a chance to discuss how they feel about the education they are receiving.

Follow-on

1. Overall, the school days in the 'What are they like?' spread get a fairly positive report. Decide what you would say about your school days if you were being interviewed. Record your thoughts. You may take the role of an existing student or of someone who left school in previous years and is looking back at their school days.

2. Provide students with a photocopy of the sheet on the following page. *Look at the nine statements. Using the Diamond 9 template, rank them in order of importance, with the most important at the top. The next two should be as important as each other, but less important than the one at the top, and so on.*

3. *Do you think that people remember their school days accurately, or are they selective in what they remember? Do you think they are more likely to remember the good things or the bad things? What do you think you would be most likely to remember? Discuss your ideas with a partner.*

4. *Can you think of any TV programmes, films or books in which the story is set within a school? How do you think former students will remember their time at that school? In the role of a former student of that school, write a few paragraphs about your school days.*

5. *If you could make one improvement to your school, what would it be? Present your idea so that it would be suitable for a class display.*

© Folens (copiable page)   **24SEVEN** Teachers' Notes

Diamond 9 – what's important in a school?

What do you think is important within a school? Rate the following in order of importance.

a. Modern, well-maintained buildings.
b. Good library facilities.
c. Well-equipped computer suite.
d. Enthusiastic and knowledgeable teachers.
e. Good academic results.
f. Varied range of out-of-school activities on offer.
g. Good discipline within the school.
h. A staff made up of different ages, races and religions.
i. Teachers who inspire and motivate their students.

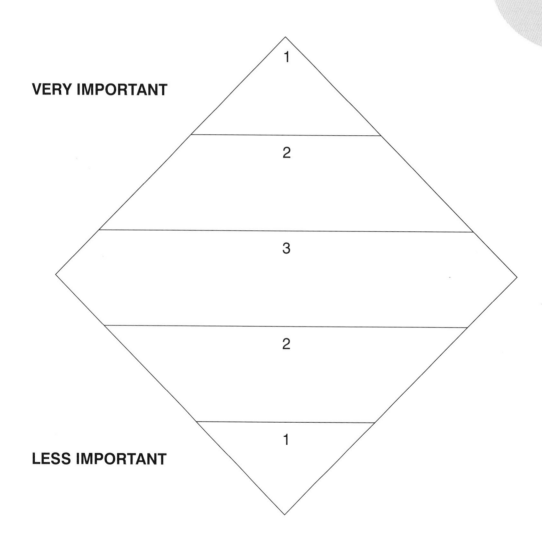

24SEVEN

Teachers' Notes

Theme: The Main Event

Topic: Star schools

Student Reference: Issue 3, pages 22-23

C/PSHE Link: PSHE 1a

Objective: To examine the range of opportunities that are available to young people at Secondary School.

Follow-on

1. Start with a brainstorming activity on the subject of 'What do you feel your school does for you?' Think about things that school does to try to improve the quality of your life as a student. You can use some of the ideas from the 'Star schools' spread to get you started if you wish.

2. What do you think are the three most important things that school does for you?

3. For each of your three answers, write a sentence to explain why each point is particularly important to you.

4. If possible, students could arrange to put these positive ideas about their school onto the school's website.

5. Lots of schools have open days of different kinds and parents' evenings. As a long-term project create some eye-catching posters that advertise things your school does really well. Collect newspaper cuttings relating to your school and anything showing students' achievements either in school or in the wider community. Your school can do great things – make sure everybody knows about it.

24SEVEN

Teachers' Notes

Theme: The Main Event

Topic: Where to next?

Student Reference: Issue 3, page 24

C/PSHE Link: PSHE 1a; Citizenship scheme of work, KS3, Unit 14

Objective: To explore students' ideas about the best type of school for them. (This topic can also offer opportunities to explore students' views on their education so far and encourage them to suggest possible improvements.)

Follow-on

1. Choose three of the statements from the 'Where to next?' spread to respond to. For each, write a brief sentence to explain why you either agree or disagree with each statement. Compare and contrast your opinions with others in your class.

2. What changes would you like to see made to education? Discuss your ideas with a partner and make a few notes as you go along. You can refer to these notes when you feed your ideas back to the rest of the class.

3. Students should spend time designing their ideal classroom. They could either draw this on A4 paper or, if possible, create something using the ICT facilities in school. They could make a scale model in a shoe box. Students should then prepare to give someone in the class a guided tour of the finished article.

Theme: The Main Event

Topic: The law says

Student Reference: Issue 3, page 25

C/PSHE Link: PSHE 1a

Objective: To discuss education and the law and how the law relating to education affects young people.

Follow-on

1. If you could make three laws relating to education, what would they be?

2. Compare and contrast your laws with those of a partner. What are the similarities and differences between your laws on education? Report your findings back to the whole class.

3. Which curriculum subjects are compulsory at Key Stage 3? Why do you think these were selected?

4. Which subjects do you think ought to be made compulsory, or made available, at Key Stage 3 which currently are not?

5. Find out what you can about Social Exclusion Units. Who are they for? How are they funded?

24SEVEN

Teachers' Notes

Theme: The Main Event

Topic: Student exclusions

Student Reference: Issue 3, pages 26-27

C/PSHE Link: PSHE 1a

Objective: To look at how and why students are excluded from school and the impact that exclusion may have on their futures.

NB Consider current policies and how they have affected your own school, before teaching this unit.

Follow-on

1. With students working in pairs, or as a whole class, go through each of the points of view raised in the student book. *How do you personally react to each one? Are the reactions stereotyped? Are you in agreement with what was said, or not?*

2. Can you think of any additional reasons why 11- to 14-year-olds have the highest exclusion rate?

3. From school policy documents, find out which offences carry a penalty of instant exclusion, either permanent or temporary. Should these offences be the same for all schools, or should school rules be tailored to fit a particular school?

4. If appropriate, students could be asked to write a brief report on what happened leading up to the time when a student at school was excluded permanently.

5. In groups, decide which offences should be dealt with by the use of either permanent or temporary exclusions.

6. Do you think students excluded from school should be educated together in a special unit? List five advantages and five disadvantages to taking this approach. What are the practicalities of this approach? Make your own conclusion – are you for or against special units?

7. What will a person excluded from school find it difficult to do? How might a person's life chances be altered if they are excluded from school?

24SEVEN

Teachers' Notes

Theme: The Main Event

Topic: Different for girls

Student Reference: Issue 3, page 28

C/PSHE Link: PSHE 1a

Objective: To look at whether or not girls are treated differently when it comes to disciplinary matters and truancy.

Follow-on

1. Do you think those who have spoken out in the 'Different for girls' spread have legitimate concerns? Are things really different for girls? Is what they are saying true or are they just complaining?

2. Which of the following two statements do you agree with, and why?
   - Disciplinary matters regarding girls should be dealt with by a female member of staff specifically trained for that role.
   - Disciplinary matters regarding any students should be dealt with by a member of staff specifically trained for that role.

   List at least five different reasons to explain why you agree with one of these statements.

3. It is often said that there is more cause for concern about the number of boys dropping out of school than the number of girls. Working with a partner, compile a brief paragraph to explain why this is the case. Share your thoughts with other members of the class.

4. Imagine that one of the girls from the spread could be assigned a home tutor. Which girl do you think should be chosen? Why?

5. Some girls, just like some boys, are not interested in school and academic achievement. What arguments would you use to persuade a 13-year-old girl that it really is worth her while to stay on at school and try to get some qualifications?

6. Does your own school have a particular policy for dealing with girls, or are boys and girls treated equally? Is the school's system fair or would you make changes to it?

7. Get on your high horse and have a good moan about girls in a letter to your local newspaper. Start with the phrase 'The trouble with girls today is that …'. This will of course be particularly challenging for the girls, so encourage them to play devil's advocate.

8. Swap letters with a partner. Challenge the statements made in your partner's letter and justify girls' lifestyle choices and actions.

24SEVEN

Teachers' Notes

Theme: The Main Event

Topic: Poverty - just an excuse?

Student Reference: Issue 3, page 29

C/PSHE Link: PSHE 1a

Objective: To examine the links between lack of money and reduced educational prospects and achievements.

Follow-on

1. "A school cannot make up for all the disadvantages that a student has to start with." What do you think of this statement? What do you think are some of the disadvantages students may face? Are the problems mainly to do with money? Are they to do with the opportunities and chances that people get? Work with a partner to come up with what you consider would be five disadvantages. Pool the class's ideas on the board.

2. What disadvantages may a student encounter that a school can put right or help with? Work with a partner to come up with five disadvantages that a school can alleviate.

3. Look up the word 'poverty' and write a definition of its meaning. What do people mean when they talk about poverty in this country? Does it have the same meaning when talking about poverty in a less developed country?

4. What are some of the implications for the future for the people born into poverty in this country? Consider the following questions:
   - What kinds of qualification might they have when they leave school?
   - What will their job prospects be?
   - Will they be able to afford their own homes?
   - Where will they live?
   - Will they be able to have the kinds of choices available to wealthier families, for example, to choose expensive organically grown food, where they go on holiday, where to live or where their own children can go to school?
   - Will they be able to get a loan from a bank?
   - What kinds of life chances will their own children have?

5. Imagine that you and a small group of your friends were given the task of doing something about poverty on a run-down estate. What would you try to do? What facilities and opportunities would you try to provide for the people living there to get them out of the cycle of poverty? For the purposes of this exercise, money is not a problem. Work together as a committee and come up with a ten-point action plan to tackle some of the worst problems. Ask each group to talk through their action plan. Encourage other students to question them about their plan.

24SEVEN

Teachers' Notes

Theme: The Main Event

Topic: Hiding in the headlines

Student Reference: Issue 3, pages 30-31

C/PSHE Link: PSHE 1a

Objective: To investigate different strategies used to combat truancy.

Follow-on

1. What do you think of each one of the ideas to combat truancy from the 'Hiding in the headlines' spread?

2. Do you think one method would be more effective than the other three or should there be a combination of methods working at once? Are incentives to stay in school and behave, unfair to those who regularly attend? If truancy is against the law, should people be looking at punishments for breaking the law, not rewards for keeping it?

3. Do you think that parents should be held responsible for their child's actions and face the consequences of either a fine or imprisonment? What are the advantages or disadvantages of a system that only holds the parents to account?

4. It is a common complaint that not enough money is invested in schools. Should time, effort and money – half a million pounds of it – be allocated to students who do not want to be in school in the first place? Justify your point of view.

5. If you were in charge of that amount of money, what would you do with it? Would you invest it in those who want to work at school or in those who need to be encouraged to stay in school? Take a class vote on this. Choose students with opposing views to try to persuade others to their way of thinking and then have a second vote.

6. What is your own school's position on truancy? Is it workable? With a partner, compile a list of five ways in which your school could reduce truancy. You will probably know of the reasons why people skip school, so be imaginative with your approach to the answer.

7. Write about a time when you, or someone you know, played truant. Try answering these questions as you write. Why did you do it? What did you do? Where did you go? Did you put yourself or others at risk? Were you caught? What were the consequences of your action?

24SEVEN

Teachers' Notes

Theme: The Main Event

Topic: Looking back – a teacher speaks out

Student Reference: Issue 3, pages 32-33

C/PSHE Link: PSHE 1a

Objective: To investigate the problems that young people have when the rules they abide by at home are at odds with those they are expected to abide by at school or elsewhere in the community.

Follow-on

1. Is it in everyone's best interests that a new student at school should be accepted 'with a clean sheet'? If you think it is, then explain why you think this. If you think it is not, then who should know what?

2. Which of these statements do you personally agree with?

   a. Guy is just a disorganised scruff.

   b. Guy hasn't got the self-discipline to sort himself out, so his school should take on this responsibility.

   c. Guy's friends and teachers should have known by his behaviour and appearance that there is a lack of support for Guy at home.

   d. In this particular case the school should have been a little more flexible and lenient.

   e. Guy is just a troublemaker. He shouldn't have been allowed in the school in the first place.

3. In small groups, come up with as many suggestions as you can to explain the conflicts Guy will have to sort out between his home life and his school life. What will his parents have to do?

4. Improvise a scene between Guy, his parents and the teacher. Try to ensure each speaker has at least four things to say. Remember, emotions are going to be running high and tempers may be short. Make your improvisations realistic. You might find this dialogue useful to get you started:

   Guy's dad: 'Make it quick. I've got a business meeting in half an hour.'

   Teacher: 'I'm glad you could come in this morning. We need to talk about Guy's recent behaviour.'

   Guy's mum: 'Everybody picks on Guy, just because he's big for his age.'

   If time permits, students could show others their role plays.

5. Parents who let their children truant from school could now face a prison sentence or a fine. What are your thoughts about introducing a similar scheme for parents and carers of children who are persistently rude, late, scruffy or antisocial? What would be the advantages and disadvantages of such a scheme?

© Folens (copiable page)

24SEVEN

Teachers' Notes

Theme: The Main Event

Topic: DIY education

Student Reference: Issue 3, pages 34-35

C/PSHE Link: PSHE 1a

Objective: To explore alternatives to mainstream education.

Follow-on

1. What are the similarities between home education and mainstream education? What are the differences? Make a list of these on the board.

2. Read through the 'DIY education' spread. What advantages does home education give this particular boy? Why can a mainstream school not provide these? Work with a partner and jot down your ideas.

3. Now, on the other side of that piece of paper, make a note of possible disadvantages of home education. What does the family do to try to overcome these disadvantages?

4. Do you think there could be a kind of halfway house between home education and state education, which might be an ideal compromise for some students? If there is, what might be on offer? Discuss your ideas with a friend.

5. For what reasons might people decide to opt for home education? Do the students themselves need to be consulted about whether or not they want to opt to return to mainstream education or should the decisions be made by the parents? Be prepared to justify your opinion.

6. Where could you go to find out more information on home education and support services linked with home education? Undertake some research and make a note of contact names and addresses.

7. Using the information from the 'DIY education' spread and from your own research, write up a six-paragraph essay which would give a reader who knew nothing about home education an insight into it. In your essay try to make 20 clear points.

8. 'DIY education' deals with a boy who opted for home education. Are his reasons for making this choice typically 'boyish'? What other reasons may boys give for choosing home education? Would girls' reasons be different? If so, how?

24SEVEN

Teachers' Notes

Theme: Friendship

Topic: Meet my mates

Student Reference: Issue 3, page 36

C/PSHE Link: PSHE 1c, 3c, 3h, 3i

Objective: To introduce students to different aspects of friendships.

Follow-on

1. Complete this sentence: 'A friend is someone who ...'.

2. List the top ten personal qualities you would like your best mate to have. Put them in order of importance. Design a poster to advertise these top ten qualities.

3. Why is it important to have friends? What do you get from friends that you do not get from your family?

4. What kinds of thing can affect friendships, either for better or worse? Can these things be controlled by the friends themselves? If so, how? Be prepared to share your ideas with other members of the class.

5. Lots of things you may do with a mate, such as watching a video or going into town, you could do on your own. Why would such activities not be as much fun on your own?

6. Most people agree that friendship is a good thing, but parents often get worried if they think their child is 'in with the wrong crowd'. Can you explain what parents are really worried about?

7. Do you think that friendships between boys are different from friendships between girls? If so, how? Is it possible for girls and boys to be friends with each other? What are the outward signs of friendships in each case? How do the friends behave towards each other? Discuss and compare your ideas with your partner.

8. "Boys and girls can never be just good friends." Prepare notes so that you can speak for one minute explaining why you agree or disagree with this statement. Develop your point of view, rather than re-state some of your initial thoughts.

© Folens (copiable page)

24SEVEN

Teachers' Notes

Theme: Friendship

Topic: Gossip at the garage

Student Reference: Issue 3, page 37

C/PSHE Link: PSHE 1c, 3c, 3h, 3i; Citizenship scheme of work, KS3, Unit 13

Objective: To look at why conflicts take place between young people and their friends and family and how some of these conflicts might be resolved.

Follow-on

1. Read through the spread 'Gossip at the garage'. As a whole class, think of four or five other statements that parents might make about their children's friends.

2. Which of these parents see their children's friendships as a positive influence? What are the positive aspects?

3. What kinds of negative influence do you think parents are worried about? Are they real or imagined?

4. Should a school try to separate students because their parents disapprove of a particular friendship? Would this solve any problems? Would it cause any further problems?

5. Working in pairs, choose two statements from the spread or make up your own and script a conversation (or an argument) between the speakers. See if you can make each speaker say at least eight things.

6. Ask students to perform their conversations. Ask for feedback from other students and ask them to comment on whether or not the scripts being performed are realistic.

7. Research details of useful local and national organisations that help parents deal with worries about their children's friends.

8. In this spread you are only given the adults' point of view. What do you think the son or daughter may say about the same friendship? Have they necessarily chosen the friendship groups or have they been engineered in some way? Imagine your teacher is a reporter and take the opportunity to provide a young person's point of view on the subject.

24SEVEN

Teachers' Notes

Theme: Friendship

Topic: Not all bad news

Student Reference: Issue 3, pages 38-39

C/PSHE Link: PSHE 1c, 3c, 3h, 3i

Objective: To explore the positive benefits of older students acting as peer supporters for younger students.

Follow-on

1. From the 'Not all bad news' spread, it is obvious that the individuals benefited from the peer support project. What do you think might be the benefits for the whole school?

2. A system like this provides lots of positive role models throughout the school. What are the advantages and benefits of this?

3. Do you think the peer supporters should reflect the school population as a whole, or should just the nicest and most caring students be used? Be prepared to justify your answer.

4. If a system like this were to be introduced into your school, how and where could peer supporters be most effectively used?

5. Do you think the system could work in any school system or would it be more effective in one type of school than another? Where do you think it would work? Why? Where do you think it might be difficult to introduce? Why?

6. Can you think why positive peer pressure does not make headline news like negative peer pressure?

7. Using between 50 and 100 words, explain why you would either like or not like to be given the opportunity to be a peer supporter.

8. Make a list of the type of problems that a peer supporter may be asked to deal with. Examples may include home sickness for a student at boarding school or problems of a student who is unable to make friends. Then write how the peer supporter could help in each case.

9. Who should support the peer supporters themselves? Is it reasonable to expect them to deal with so many problems?

10. As a peer supporter, you notice that a 12-year-old girl is looking very unhappy. She tells you her parents have just separated, but makes you promise not to tell anyone. What should you do?

© Folens (copiable page)

24SEVEN

Teachers' Notes

Theme: Friendship

Topic: Phone up for a little friendly advice

Student Reference: Issue 3, pages 40-41

C/PSHE Link: PSHE 1c, 3c, 3h, 3i

Objective: To give students the chance to discuss various problems that may arise between friends. To prompt students to consider whether they can resolve the issues, or whether a little help from another source is needed.

Follow-on

1. Working in pairs, decide what advice you would give to each of the callers on the 'Phone up for a little friendly advice' spread. What help would you offer in order to resolve the situation successfully? Is it always possible to do that? Is there only one possible course of action?

2. Would it be possible for the callers in each situation to decide that the friendship just wasn't worth continuing with? If not, why not? Discuss your ideas with a partner and feed your ideas back to the whole class.

3. Which situations would need more than just the friends themselves involved in sorting out the problem? Who else should become involved? When should they become involved?

4. It is very unlikely that the situations outlined on this spread would have occurred with children who were aged seven or eight. Why not? What does this say about the nature of the problems you may encounter in your relationships? What other influences and pressures are showing themselves?

5. Improvise, in pairs, a scene between the two friends in message 1 or message 4. Let the caller start the improvisation with the line, 'Look. It's about time we got something straight here.' Try to make the scene last at least 90 seconds. Script the scene when you feel confident that you have some effective lines.

6. After you have performed the improvisation, discuss with your partner how each of the characters is probably feeling as the scene goes on. Are they angry? Annoyed? Jealous? Confused? Would now be a good time to make an important decision?

7. If you had received these messages and had to put them into some sort of priority order, write down what that order would be and how you would come to that decision.

24SEVEN

Teachers' Notes

Theme: Friendship

Topic: A bridge too far

Student Reference: Issue 3, pages 42-43

C/PSHE Link: PSHE 1c, 3c, 3h, 3i

Objective: To give students the chance to look at some of the negative influences of certain types of friendship. (There may be opportunities to discuss similar kinds of situations that have been reported in your local area.)

Follow-on

1. Andy and Pete seem very different in temperament and outlook on life. Can you suggest what they see in each other as friends? What does one give the other? Who is in control?

2. Give some reasons why you think Andy does what Pete says, even though he has reservations about it. What do you think Andy is trying to prove?

3. What do you think makes Andy decide that enough is enough? What is he afraid of?

4. Do you think Pete intended to throw a shopping trolley off the bridge, or was it a result of the boys getting carried away? Be prepared to explain the answer you give.

5. In what ways has Andy acted like a good friend to Pete? What has he done with him and for him that you would expect of a good friend?

6. Both boys will have to make a statement to the police about what happened. Using up to 200 words, write down what you think either Pete's or Andy's statement will be. Your statement must include:
   - details of events leading up to the trolley being lifted onto the railings
   - exactly what happened to make the trolley fall onto the carriageway, from your point of view.

   Read out a sample of these statements and ask students to decide whose story is the more convincing.

7. Three months later, how do you think Andy will feel about Pete? What positive things could come out of this bad experience?

8. Can you think of examples from real life where young people have got carried away with something that started as a joke and led to them doing something terrible?

© Folens (copiable page)   **24SEVEN** Teachers' Notes   29

24SEVEN

Teachers' Notes

Theme: Friendship

Topic: Doer or doormat?

Student Reference: Issue 3, pages 44–45

C/PSHE Link: PSHE 1c, 3c, 3h, 3i

Objective: To make students aware that not all friendships are based on equality. To highlight how different friendships are established and sustained, and why it is important to be able to negotiate within a relationship.

Follow-on

1. In small groups, give four definitions of each of the following personality traits:
   - being aggressive is …
   - being passive is …
   - being manipulative is …
   - being assertive is …

   Use the 'Doer or doormat?' spread to help you.

2. Which type of friend would you most like to have? Be prepared to explain your choice.

3. Imagine that, completely by accident, you have left your friend's name off an invitation list to a party at your house. How do you think an aggressive friend will deal with the situation when he or she finds out?

4. Using the same scenario as before, decide how an assertive, a passive and a manipulative friend would handle the situation.

5. Choose one type of friend from the four categories and improvise the scene between you and them. How can you resolve the situation?

6. What might happen to you if you let yourself be bullied or emotionally blackmailed into letting your friend have their own way?

7. Which type of friend do you think you are? Which type of friend would you most like to be? You do not have to tell anyone, but you could think about the ways in which you might have to change your behaviour if you want a fairer friendship.

8. Think of some characters from books, TV or film and try to categorise their personality traits. Write a brief paragraph to describe an incident which illustrates this aspect of their personality.

24SEVEN

Teachers' Notes

Theme:	Friendship
Topic:	Magic mates
Student Reference:	Issue 3, page 46
C/PSHE Link:	PSHE 1c, 3c, 3h, 3i
Objective:	To explore what makes a friend so special and so important to our health and happiness.

Follow-on

1. Answer the question 'What's the best thing your mate has ever done?'
2. Create a cartoon strip showing your answer to this question. If any of the incidents are related to something that happened in school, you could try to get the best ones printed in your school magazine.
3. Describe how it made you feel when someone did something really special on your behalf. How do you think your friend felt about what they had done for you? Make a list of the positive emotions connected with friendship.
4. Write a definition of the word 'friendship'. Display definitions around the class.

Theme:	Friendship
Topic:	Friends 4 ever?
Student Reference:	Issue 3, page 47
C/PSHE Link:	PSHE 1c, 3c, 3h, 3i
Objective:	To look at the ups and downs of friendship and to consider how to resolve problems before they escalate.

Follow-on

1. Think back to when you have had an argument with a friend. What had you fallen out about?
2. Are there differences between what causes boys to fall out and what causes girls to fall out? If so, what are they? Why do you think these differences exist?
3. With a partner, go through each statement on the 'Friends 4 ever?' spread and decide if the friendship could be mended. What would have to be said or done to try to smooth things out? Who would have to take the first steps towards reconciliation?
4. In most of the cases in this spread, the falling out has been the end result of something that has been going on for a short while. What might have been said or done earlier to prevent the break up?
5. These fallings out probably wouldn't have occurred if the people involved were under the age of ten. Why should these problems start to occur in the 11–14 age range?
6. Which of the arguments in this spread would be easier for you to forgive and forget? Put them in rank order; number 1 should be the easiest to forgive.

© Folens (copiable page)

24SEVEN

Teachers' Notes

Theme: Friendship

Topic: Focus v friendship: Emma's story

Student Reference: Issue 3, page 48

C/PSHE Link: PSHE 1c, 3c, 3h, 3i

Objective: To explore the dilemmas students face when they try to balance their own personal goals with the demands of their school life.

Follow-on

1. Emma does not seem worried about the way her friendships in school are developing; do you think she should be?

2. As they get older how might Emma's school friends start treating her, if she has nothing to do with them outside school?

3. Emma is absolutely focused on her training. How can her friends support her? How can she support her friends? In what ways could she be storing up trouble for herself in the long run by being so single-minded?

4. Should students with particular talents be educated in special schools rather than in mainstream schools? What are the advantages and disadvantages of each system for a student like Emma?

5. "I want to be a champion. If that means sacrificing school friendships then I will make that sacrifice." Do you agree or disagree with this statement? In groups, take a vote on whether or not you agree. Elect a spokesperson to feed your results back to the class with your reasons for making that choice.

6. Do you think the same problems would arise with a 12-year-old boy who was brilliant at football? Explain your answer.

7. Write a short letter to Emma, outlining your thoughts and feelings about how she is managing her friendships. Should she make compromises? Is the balance of her life wrong? Do you fully support her ambition? If she was your friend, how would you deal with this situation?

8. Should schools be concerned with students' friendships and personal and social development? Or, should schools just be concerned with sporting and academic achievement? If possible, students could interview the Headteacher to find out their point of view.